Ultimate
Aptitude Tests

Ultimate
Aptitude Tests

Assess your potential with aptitude, motivational and personality tests

Jim Barrett

KOGAN PAGE

First Indian Edition 2009

Kogan Page India Private Limited
4737/23 Ansari Road,
Daryaganj
New Delhi 110 002

This edition is for sale in the Indian subcontinent only. Not for export elsewhere.

ISBN-10: 81-7554-468-6
ISBN-13: 978-81-7554-468-0

Published by Vinod Vasishtha for Kogan Page India Private Limited,
4737/23, Ansari Road, Daryaganj, New Delhi 110 002.

Printed and bound by Raj Press, R-3, Inderpuri, New Delhi - 110 012.

Contents

Introduction

The aptitude tests in this book are wide ranging and cover the types of tests found in 'real' assessment and selection situations. They are suited to people at secondary school, college and in employment.

What are aptitude tests?

Aptitude tests aim to measure the direction and power of a person's intelligence. Properly devised aptitude tests like those in this book use scientific methods to ensure consistency of results and accurate comparison of one result with another. You can then predict what your competencies are likely to be. Obviously, if a test is not predictive there is little point in using it.

When and why are aptitude tests used?

It is becoming routine for organizations to use tests to select externally as well as internally. Why internally, when you might suppose that a person's abilities and characteristics are already well known? Here are some of the advantages:

- to create awareness of further potential for development in the person's present job;
- as a means of assessing suitability for alternative functional opportunities within the same organization;
- in competition with external applicants, to deliberately 'test the market', that is, to ensure that the quality of internal staff is keeping pace with what is happening in other, possibly rival, organizations;
- as a way of validating training programmes;
- for purposes of career guidance and counselling.

Why are aptitude tests useful?

Aptitude tests are just like any other tools that can increase efficiency and productivity. There is substantial risk attached to selecting or developing people who turn out to be unsuitable, and the financial costs attached to wrong decisions about employment can be considerable.

Testing enables many of the aims of organizations that, ultimately, are to do with getting the best results from their people, for example:

- to obtain the most competent students or staff and to develop that competence in order to make fullest use of each person's contribution;
- to reduce the risk of people leaving, since it makes sense to develop staff, where possible, if they have talents that can be extended;
- to be proactive in discovering potential in staff who may not be aware of it themselves;
- to develop relevant training programmes, either because the tests check on the effectiveness of training or because they help to make sure that training is directed at those most likely to benefit from it;
- to obtain increased staff satisfaction as the result of using tests, since they are not used to judge performance in the present job, but to reveal possible opportunities.

So, provided aptitude tests are used properly there is 'nothing to lose, but everything to gain' by the use of tests.

Anything that will decrease costs and increase the probability of success will be taken seriously by an organization. This has led many organizations to investigate numerous methods, including graphology and astrology, but it is only the psychometric test method that can be shown to be consistently accurate, going beyond guesswork or 'gazing into a crystal ball'!

How accurate are the tests?

Predictive validity simply asks whether any kind of test, assertion or forecast is accurate. A ruler is a common measure of scale; a ruler measures distances of height, length or width. In the case of aptitude tests, the type of ruler used is a scale to measure *validity*.

The scale of *validity* is said to be zero if a forecast is correct only 50 per cent of the time. This is equivalent to 'tossing a coin' and obtaining heads or tails. If you could predict accurately every time the coin was tossed whether it would land heads or tails, then you would be predicting with perfect accuracy. In this case the *validity* would be 100 per cent.

Any test or forecast that is better than chance may be useful. That is why we ask the advice of people we presume to be wise; as they have 'done it before' we hope they will increase our chances of making a good choice. The trouble with using a 'wise person' is, of course, that what they say is not scientific, whatever skill they have being limited to their own experience.

It is very difficult indeed to obtain a perfect prediction, though in some sciences and industries we are shocked when we learn that predictions are imperfect. For example, a prediction that an aircraft will not crash is very close to 100 per cent. Aircraft safety needs to be an almost perfect prediction as we would probably not ride in an aircraft if we thought that it had any chance of crashing. In fact, *predictive validity* in this area is so high that most of us can put it out of our mind. Yet, unfortunately, crashes occur, reminding us that we do have to live with less than perfect prediction in this world.

Predicting human performance is extremely complicated, much more difficult than predicting what will happen to machines. This is why predictions based upon tests, even those that are well researched, commonly fall well short of a perfect 100 per cent. This may be for two reasons: 1) there may be circumstances related to the test itself, including its administration or interpretation that undermine its predictive value; 2) there may be circumstances around the person, or subject, who has taken the test that alter the chance of the test being predictive, such as altered social or emotional circumstances.

Among selection devices, graphology, astrology and similar methods are no better than chance. Although individuals who claim to have special insight or powers of divination have been employed by organizations to help make selection of staff, their success has probably depended more on their intuition as an interviewer than any valid method in their prognostications. In contrast, aptitude tests are:

- an efficient way of collecting information;
- objective, as the information is difficult to obtain by any other method; for example, where an interview question might be 'How good is your maths?', a test score can say precisely how good a person is;
- comparative: individuals can be compared directly with a relevant group;
- a better way of predicting success or satisfaction at various jobs than other selection devices.

What do the tests measure?

The psychometric tests used in this book have a number of advantages. They give an indication of abstract and practical mental capacity in six significant areas. They are varied enough to give an indication of potential as well as present attainment. As they have been standardized on the same population it is possible to obtain an estimate of how much better, or worse, you may be on one test as opposed to another.

It is obvious that people do have aptitudes that lead them to become better in one area of study or area of work than others. No other explanation fits our observation of the range and diversity of talent people have and why, in our own case, we know we have strengths and weaknesses.

Most people are aware of their strengths and weaknesses, but often over- or underestimate themselves. Sometimes they have never had cause to use a particular talent and thus have never become aware that it lies dormant in them. Organizations may also use tests to establish the presence of characteristics they think are important because they distrust conventional examination results or do not think that those results are appropriate for various reasons.

It is worth remembering that tests of one kind or another are being used all the time, as we constantly judge people against our experience. Sometimes we get it right, sometimes we don't. Tests should help us to get it right more often, though nothing can ever be asserted with complete finality.

What it is possible to do with psychometric tests is to assert a probability, for example the probability that a particular event will happen is less than one in a hundred or one in a thousand, and so on. This is the nature of both statistics and human potential, where we are dealing with probabilities, not certainties.

Therefore, we have to try to estimate how certain, or uncertain, we are when we use tests. For example, just because someone has not obtained a certain level on a test, it does not mean that they cannot succeed in a particular job. So, how likely is it that an individual might succeed or fail? If it can be shown that only 5 per cent of people who obtain that a particular score are likely to be successful, then an organization may be justified in giving the job to someone who has a 95 per cent chance of being successful.

What is the difference between 'aptitudes' and 'abilities'?

Aptitudes should not be confused with abilities. Present skills and capabilities are not aptitudes. Aptitudes are about 'potential', which is not necessarily realized at the present time. It is like a natural intelligence. Many tests show a mixture of both ability and aptitude – ability to understand what the test requires and aptitude to perform at something for which a person may not as yet have any prior experience.

It is reasonable to measure aptitude only when it is assumed that people taking the test have had sufficient chance to develop the same ability. For example, there would be little point in giving a test of English vocabulary to a candidate who spoke very little English if all the other candidates were native English speakers. On the other hand, such tests are routinely used in teaching English as a foreign language, where applicants' level of English needs to be known.

Where ability is not required and testers want to look at some form of potential that may be exploited, tests become more abstract, for example reducing the need for vocabulary or numerical skills. This is how aptitude tests discover people with potential beyond the skills that have emerged thus far!

In summary, aptitude tests allow us to:

- Look at potential in a similar way for everybody. They attempt to put everybody on an 'equal playing field'. Even though there may never be such a thing, because life is rarely like that, there are advantages in seeing what happens when we try.

  They are a way of attempting to 'take stock' of something that is usually affected, contaminated and distorted by so many other variables, in particular educational disadvantage or prejudice.
- They are a means of trying to ensure that there is some opportunity for people to demonstrate the resources they have.
- They can investigate whether there is potential that people are not aware of. Often, the discovery of potential leads to the development of new interests or a fuller personal realization.

Comparing your aptitude on different tests

An individual's aptitudes only make sense in relation to others. Therefore, the tests in this book have been devised, using standard procedures, to compare you as far as possible with everybody else. Otherwise, you cannot say with any certainty that you are better at words than numbers.

You also have to make sure certain conditions are met so that the tests work as accurately as possible and to give yourself the same chance as everybody else. This is not literally possible; no two people can ever be in exactly the same situation when they are tested: there are just too many physical, social and emotional variables. However, as far as possible, disadvantageous factors must be removed. For example, make sure you:

- are not distracted;
- are comfortable;
- are prepared;

- are clear about the instructions;
- are timed accurately;
- have the necessary external resources;
- are treated as fairly as everyone else.

There is a case for saying that the situation in which the same test is taken is almost bound to be unique, as it may be impossible to nullify the effect of so many variables. However, you must do the best you can.

You can think of reducing many of the major adverse variables yourself, such as poor lighting, cramped conditions, intimidation and so on, but you cannot always think of everything. Therefore, it is wise to prepare for testing in advance by dealing with anything that might be distracting and making sure that you have everything you need to do the test.

Interpreting your test results

Proper interpretation of tests is the province of an expert, someone who knows how the test must be administered, knows about the test itself and what test scores mean, and has had sufficient practice in using tests. However, this book is designed to assist you to use them properly so that you can obtain meaningful results from doing them. Notes on the purpose of each test precede each section. At the end of the book you will find instructions and a chart to assist you in calculating your intelligence quotient or IQ. With this information you will be able to gain some insight into your intellectual strengths and how you may be able to use them.

Part 1

Abstract visual tests

The three tests in this section are of a type long regarded as being the 'purest' means of measuring basic intelligence, that is, the natural ability you were born with. This is because the tests are only minimally dependent upon prior learning or past skills. In particular, there is no verbal or numerical processing involved. They are thus good indicators of whether a person's educational attainments are keeping pace with the level of potential indicated by the level shown on these tests. If not, it will often be worth using remedial or training programmes to raise a person's performance to the level that the measure of their basic intelligence indicates they are capable of.

Test 1, Constructs, measures an aptitude for seeing around things, from different angles and sides and in different ways. Put like this, you may appreciate that these qualities are relevant to a broad spectrum of careers demanding intellectual flexibility and depth. For reasons that are not fully understood, people with this type of ability are usually as good at working out social issues as they are factual ones.

Test 2, Sequences, does not have the multi-dimensional element of Constructs, but it requires a more linear, logical approach. An intensity of concentration is required to maintain the thread of clues in order to arrive at the end result. Like the other tests in this section, Sequences is a demanding task often revealing a long-term potential that may not be apparent in a young person but comes out in adulthood.

Test 3, Perceptual, requires a deductive approach to problem solving, an aptitude for grasping the situation and organizing its essential elements in order to draw a conclusion. People who do well on this test often have a leaning towards science, including social science, possibly because it highlights their ability in handling abstract relevant information.

Test 1

Constructs

In this test you have to imagine how a design would look when it is folded up to make a cube (or box). In each case you are given a plan of an unfolded cube and your job is to fold it together 'in your mind'. For example:

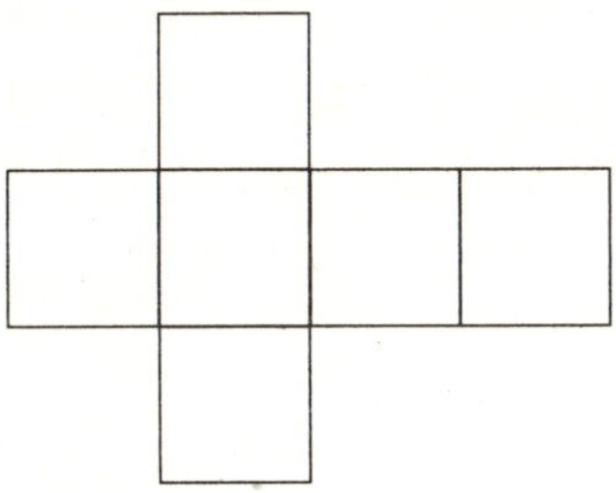

becomes

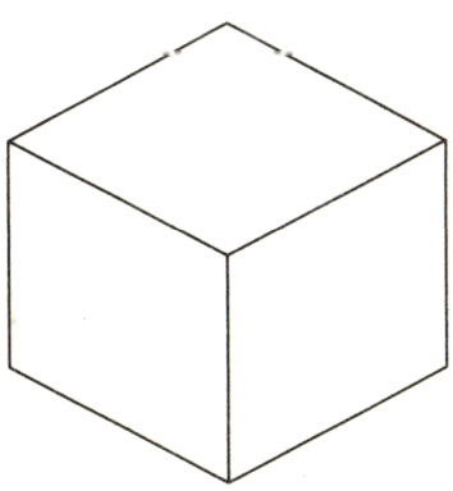

To the right of each plan, you are shown four cubes. For each item, write 'Y' for Yes or mark a tick if you think the cube is made from the plan, and write 'N' for No or make a cross if you think it could not be made from the plan. If you want to change your answer, rub out and clearly tick your preference. Examples 1) and 2) have been done to show you how. If this is not your book, please mark your answers on a piece of spare paper.

Example 1

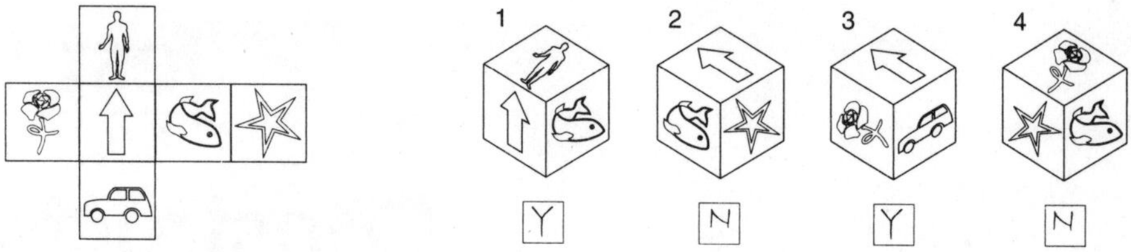

Example 2

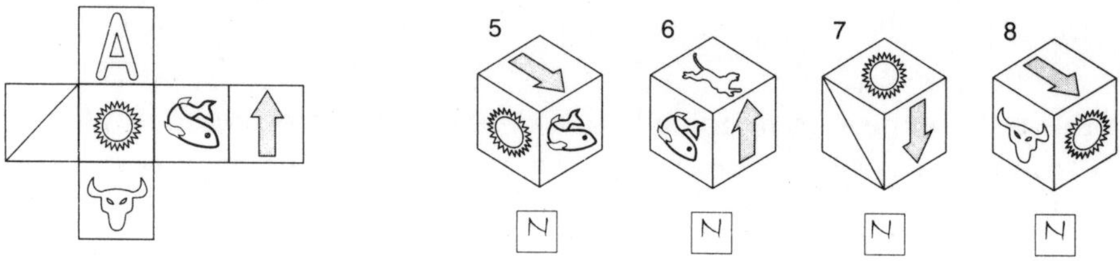

If you want, you can have paper and a pencil ready in case you want to draw out the figures. You have to work as quickly and as accurately as you can. Remember, if this is not your book, record your answers on a separate sheet of paper. Timing yourself on this test will give you the best estimate of your aptitude and allows the most accurate comparison between your results and those of others, as well as comparing your performance on other tests. If you are doing the test only to gain familiarity with this type of test you can, of course, spend as much time as you like on the test.

Timed test: 8 minutes

A

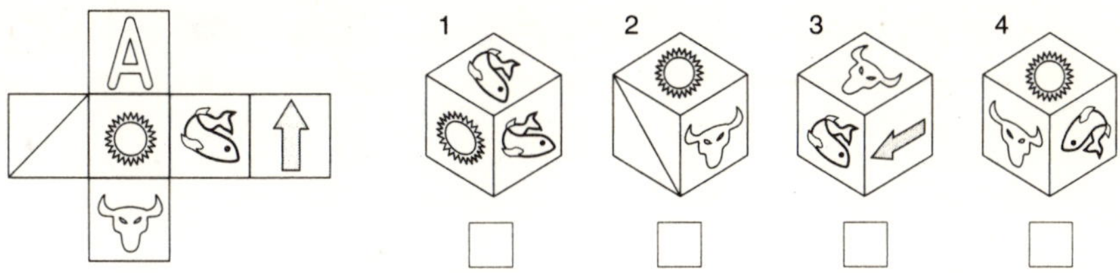

B

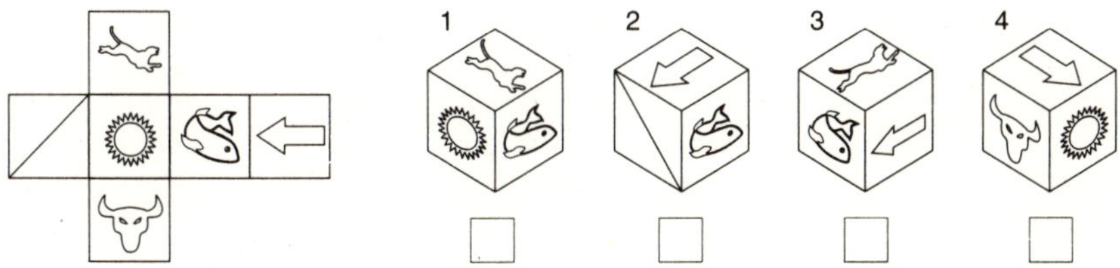

C

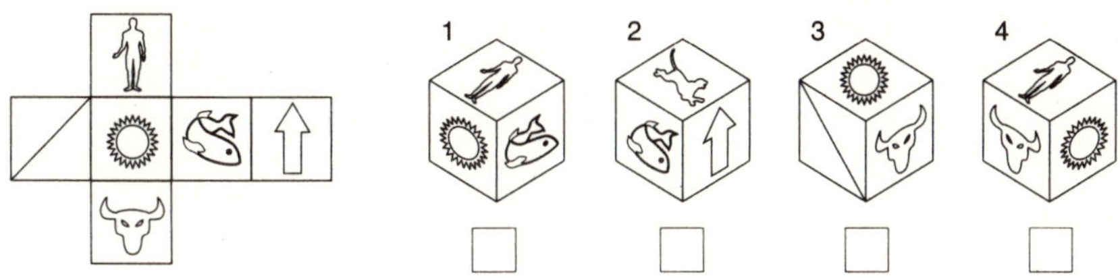

D

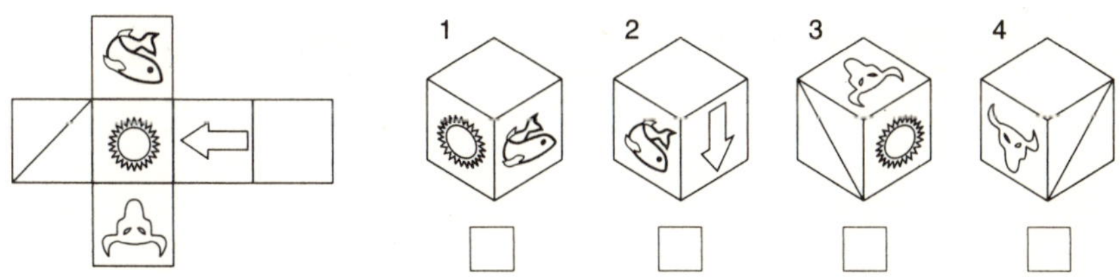

E

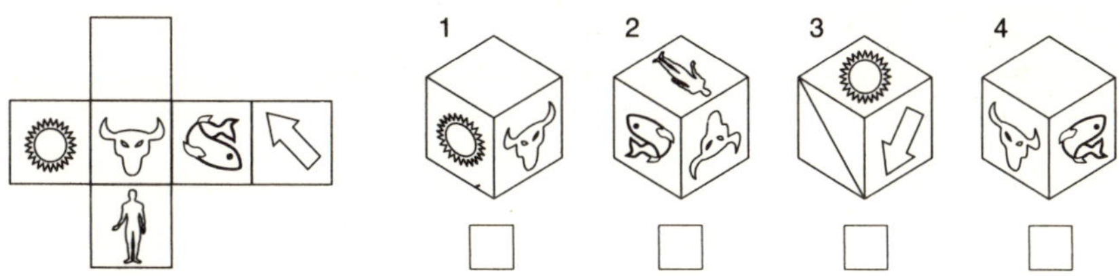

F

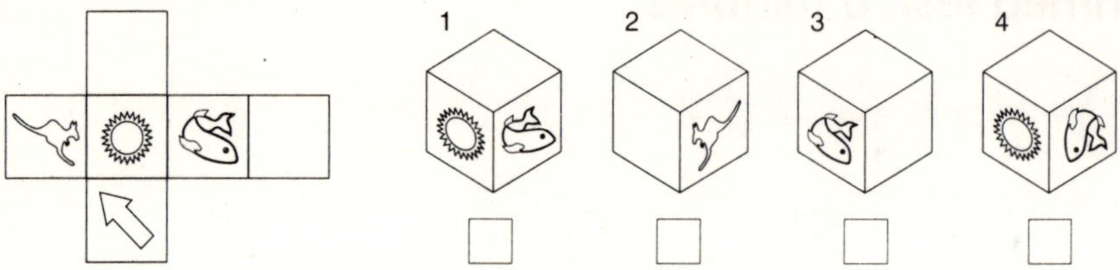

G

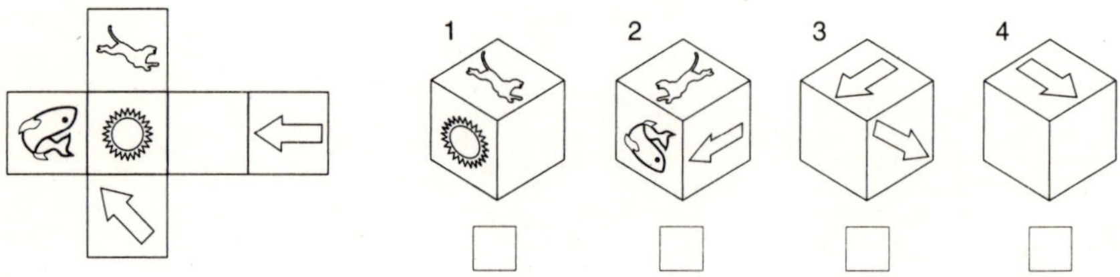

H

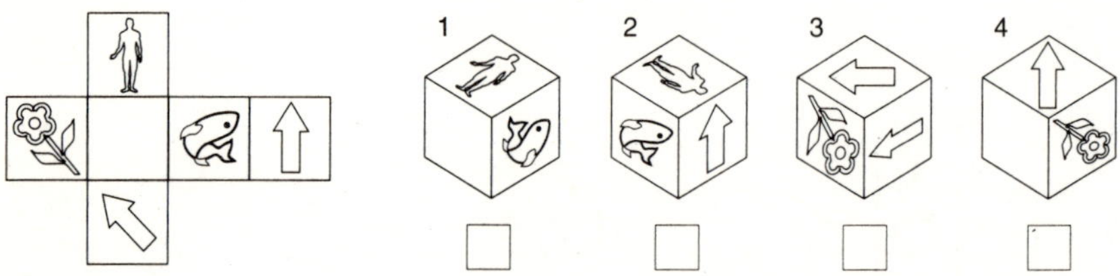

I

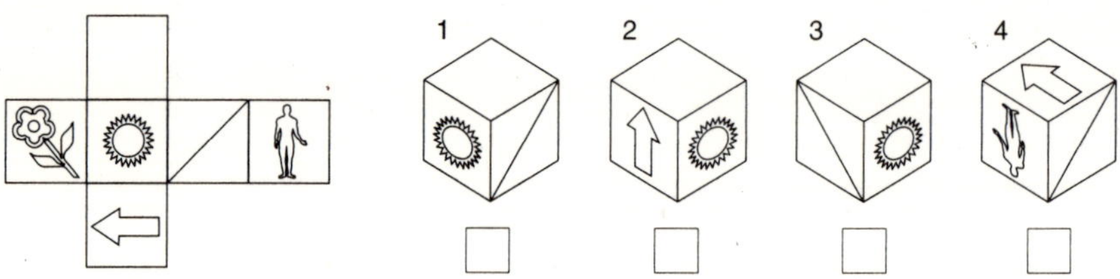

J

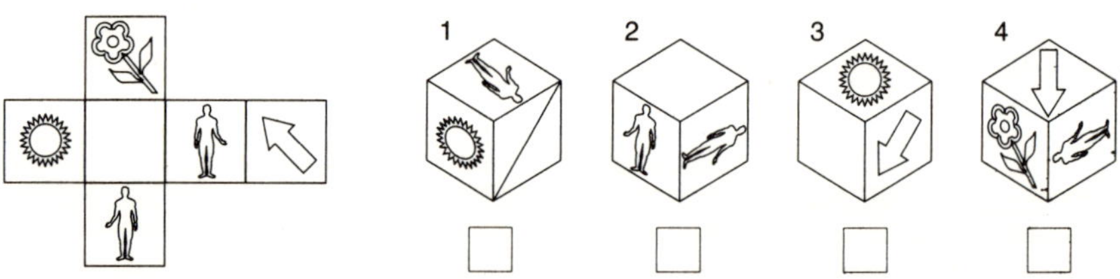

K

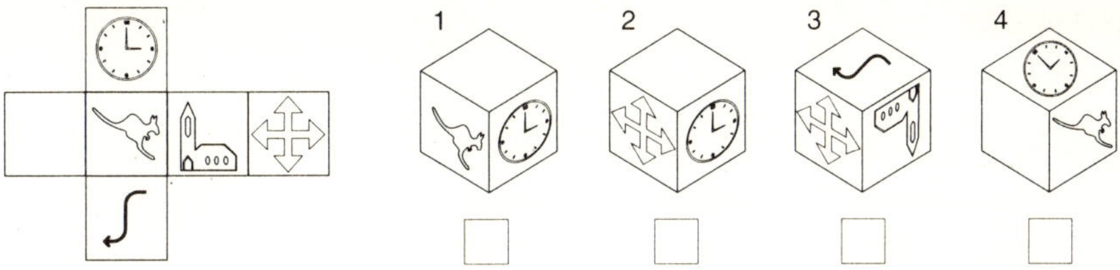

L

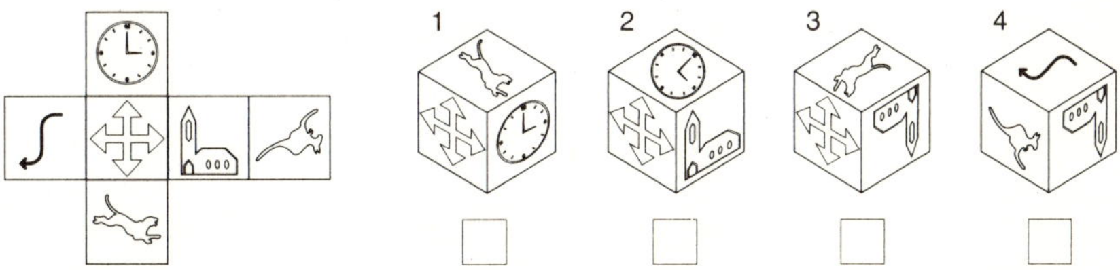

M

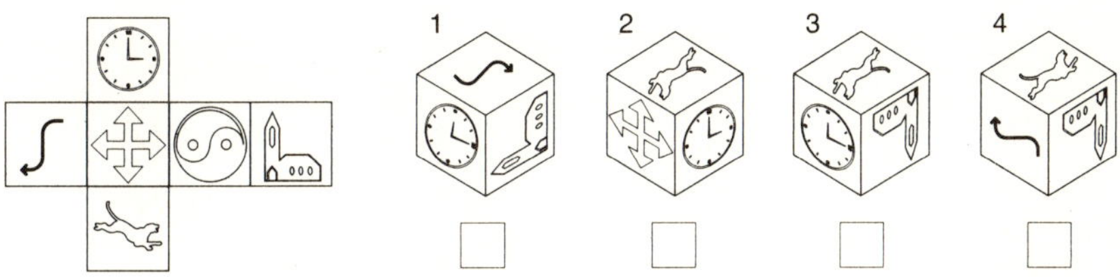

N

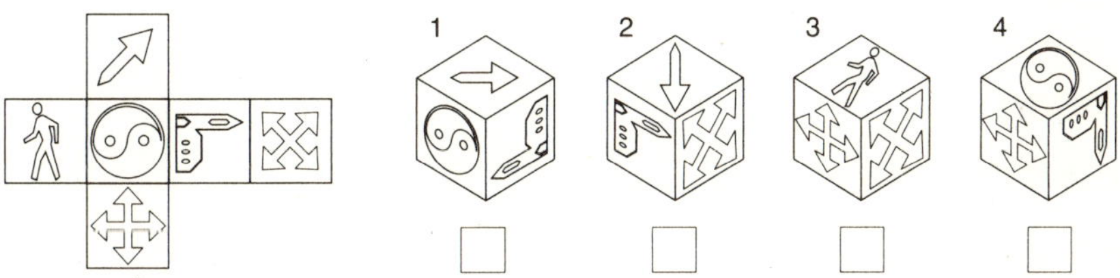

O

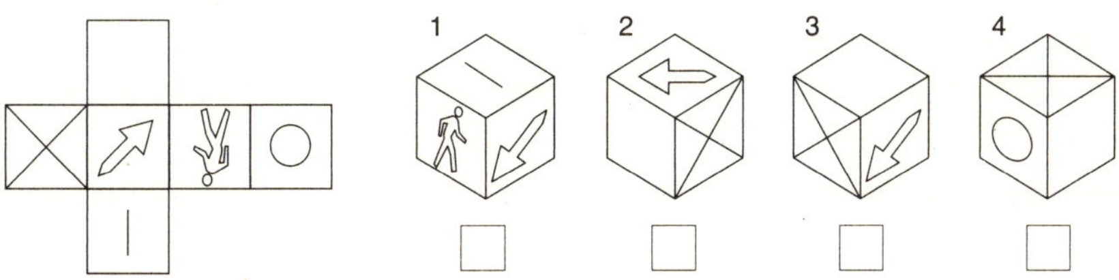

Answers

A	1. N	2. Y	3. N	4. Y
B	1. Y	2. N	3. Y	4. N
C	1. Y	2. N	3. Y	4. N
D	1. N	2. Y	3. N	4. N
E	1. Y	2. Y	3. Y	4. Y
F	1. Y	2. N	3. Y	4. N
G	1. Y	2. N	3. Y	4. N
H	1. N	2. N	3. N	4. N
I	1. Y	2. N	3. N	4. Y
J	1. N	2. Y	3. N	4. Y
K	1. N	2. N	3. Y	4. Y
L	1. N	2. Y	3. N	4. N
M	1. Y	2. N	3. N	4. N
N	1. N	2. Y	3. N	4. Y
O	1. Y	2. Y	3. N	4. N

Scoring

Number right minus number wrong = __________

Plus 4 aged under 16, plus 2 if aged 17–20 + __________

Score on the test = __________

Use the following table to convert your test score to a score out of 10 or 'sten score'. You can then enter your 'sten score' in the chart on page 200.

Test score	1–15	16–20	21–25	26–30	31–35	36–40	41–43	44–46	47–49	50+
Sten score	1	2	3	4	5	6	7	8	9	10

Test 2

Sequences

You are given a string of shapes. You have to work out which two shapes are missing from the string. The missing shapes have been replaced with a 1 and a 2. Choose the correct answers from the possible answers provided on the page. Write in the correct letter which goes with the missing shape. There is space to write in your answers on the right of the page.
Possible answers:

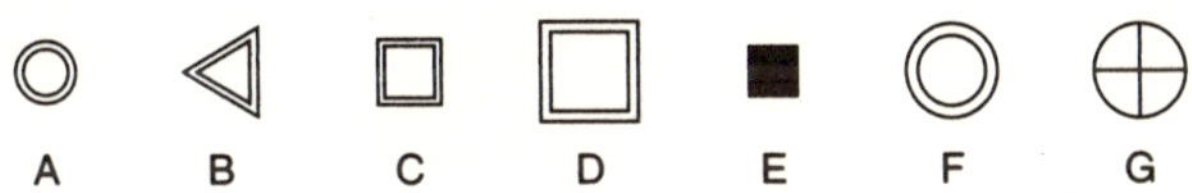

Example 1

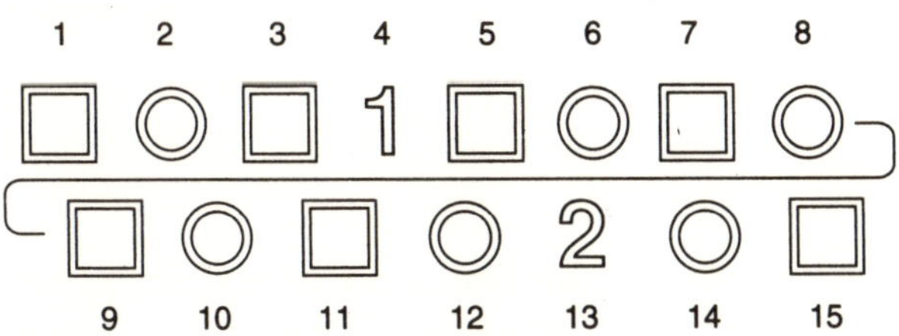

Answers
1=F
2=D

Example 2

Answers

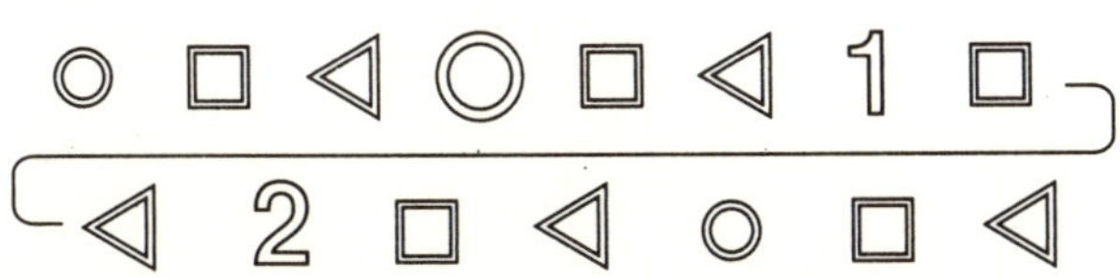

1=A
2=F

In Example 1, there is a sequence of alternate squares and circles. The fourth in the sequence is a missing circle, so F is correct from the possible answers. Number 13 in the sequence, where a 2 has been placed, should have a square, so the correct answer is D.

In Example 2, the sequence is triangle, circle, square. A small, white circle would go where the 1 has been placed, so the correct answer is A. In the sequence, the circles are alternately small and large. A large circle would go where the 2 has been placed, so the correct answer is F.

The real test is done in just this way. Find the correct answer from those given on each page and write the letter in the space provided for answers. Both parts must be correct to score.

Do not mark this book if it is not your own, but record your answers and any working out you need to do on separate paper. If you wish to get an accurate idea of your aptitude, record the number of the question you are on after exactly 15 minutes. Otherwise, take as long as you wish to complete the items.

Timed test: 15 minutes

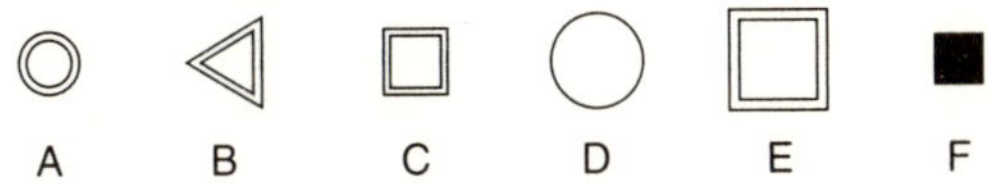

1.

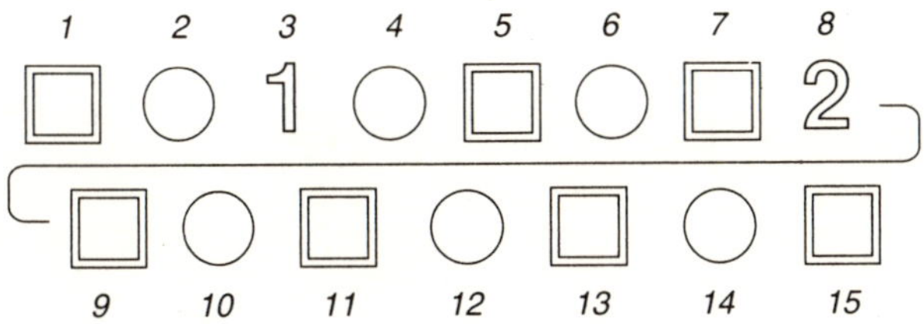

1 =
2 =

2.

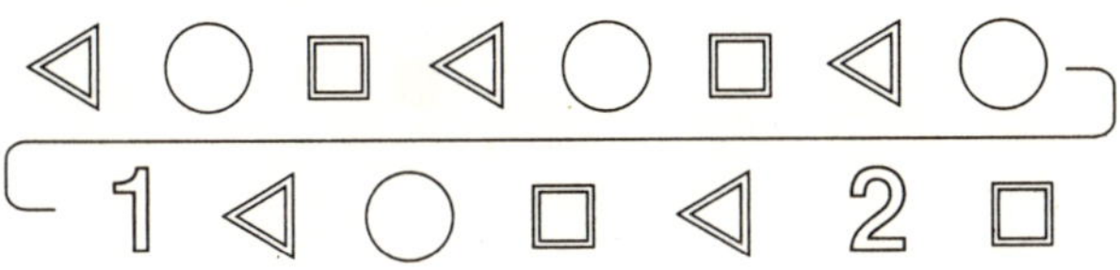

1 =
2 =

3.

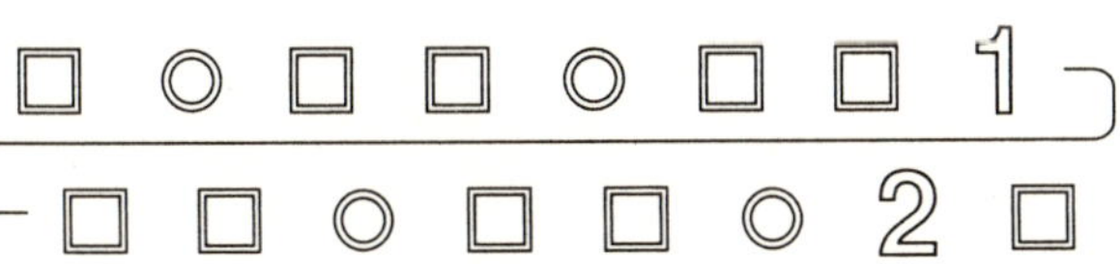

1 =
2 =

4.

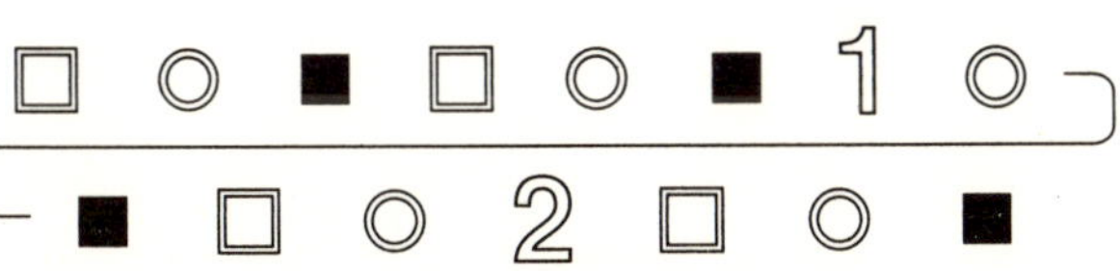

1 =
2 =

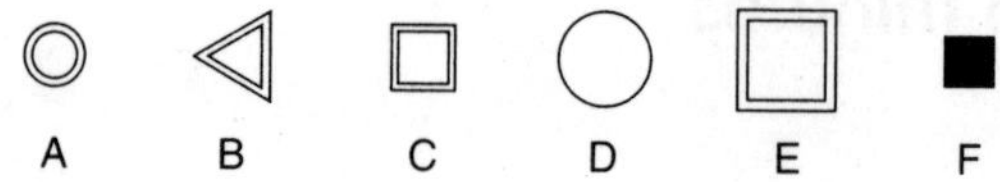

5.

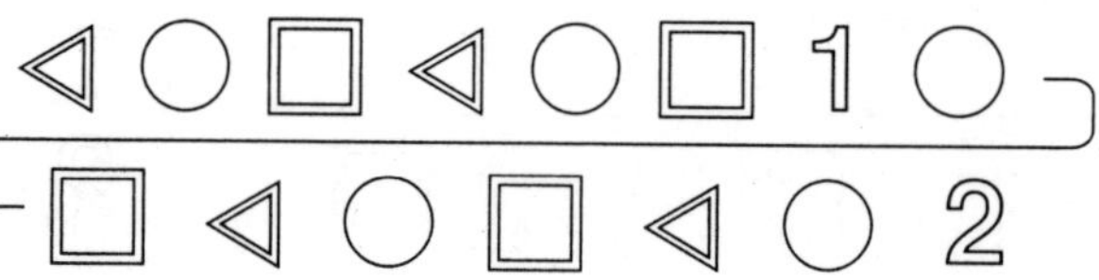

1 =

2 =

6.

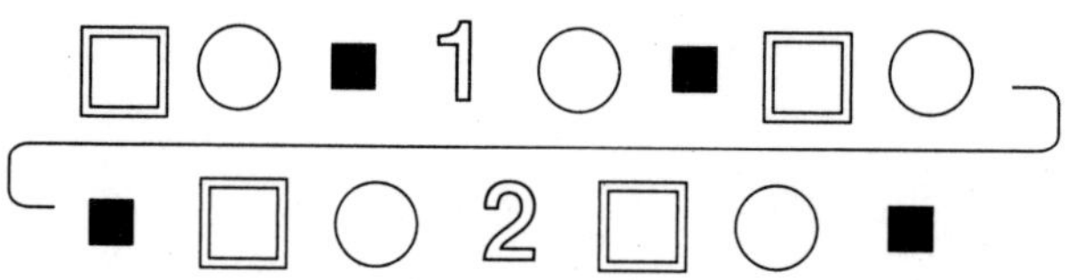

1 =

2 =

7.

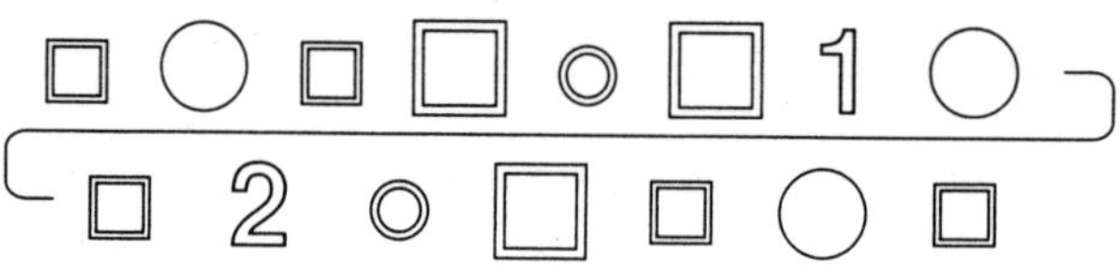

1 =

2 =

8.

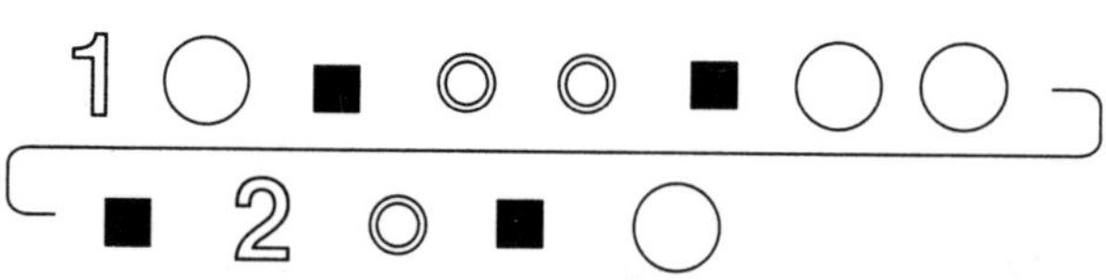

1 =

2 =

9.

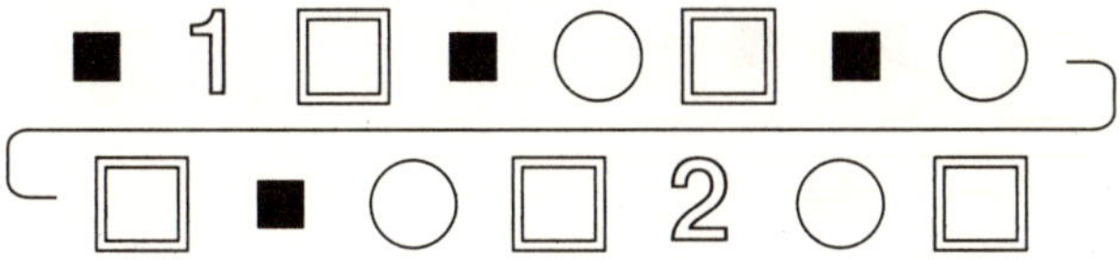

1 =
2 =

10.

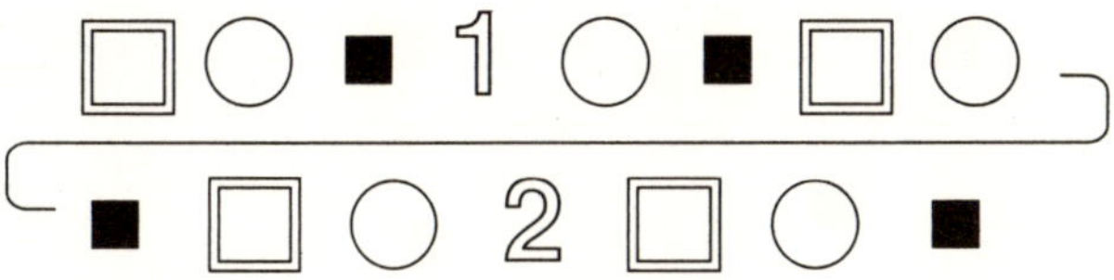

1 =
2 =

11.

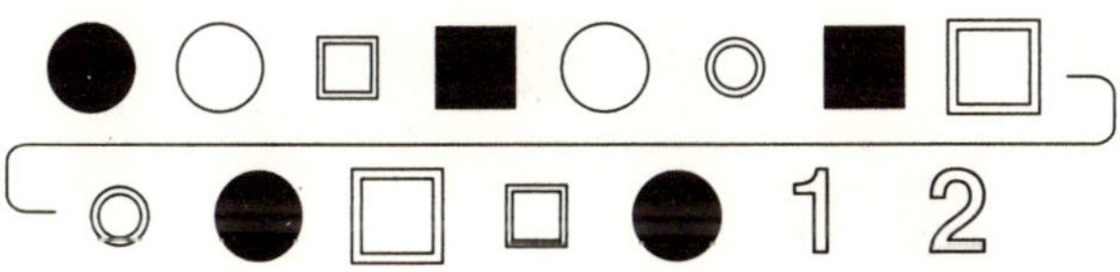

1 =
2 =

12.

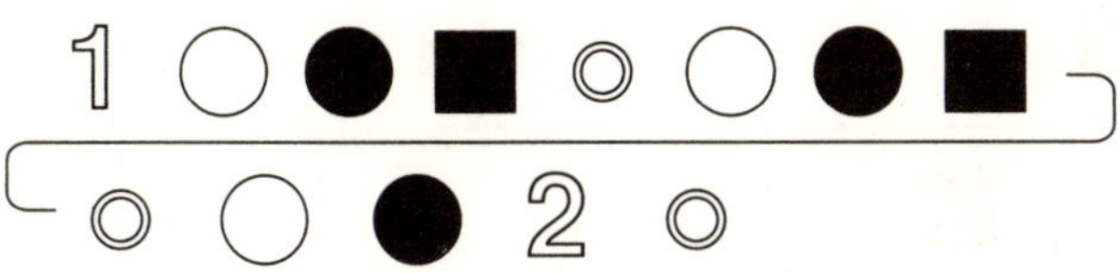

1 =
2 =

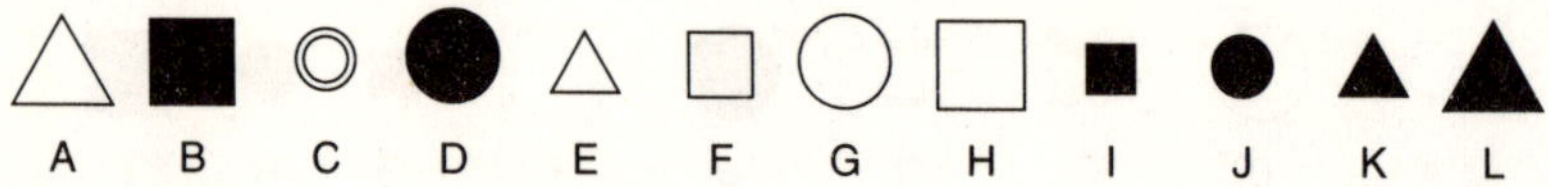

13. 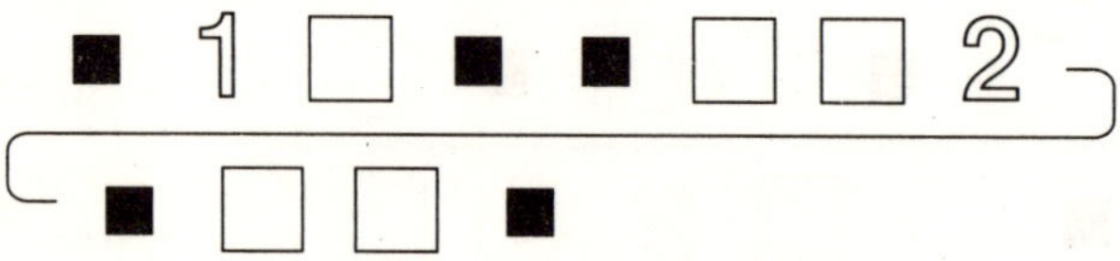

1 =
2 =

14. 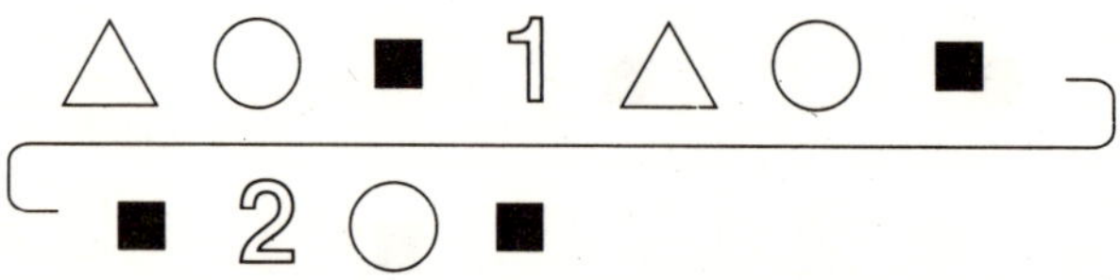

1 =
2 =

15. 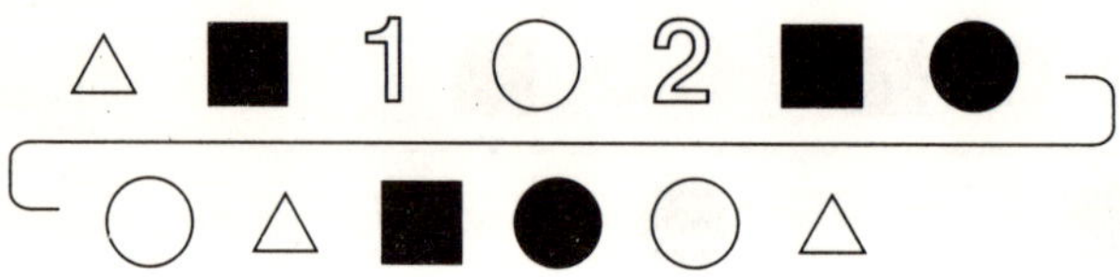

1 =
2 =

16. 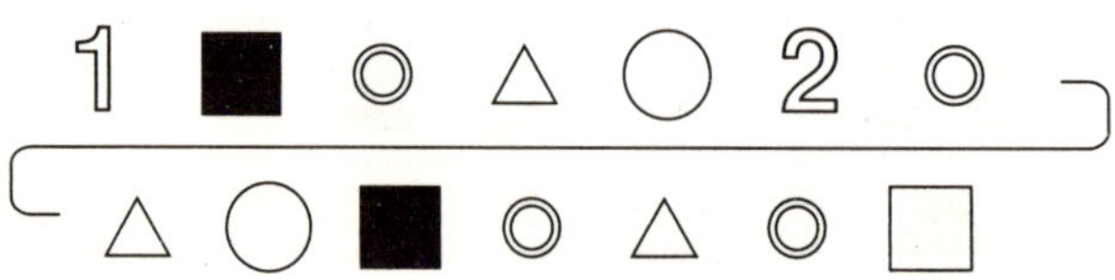

1 =
2 =

A B C D E F G H I J K L

17.

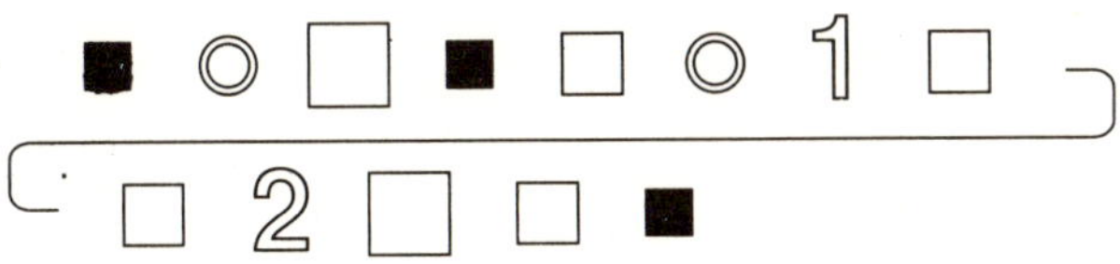

1 =

2 =

18.

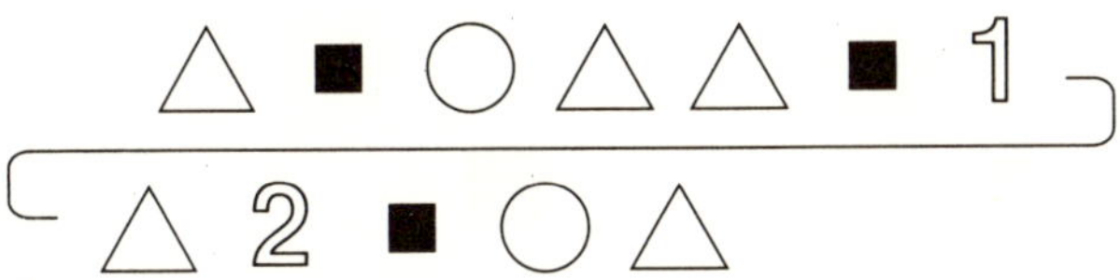

1 =

2 =

19.

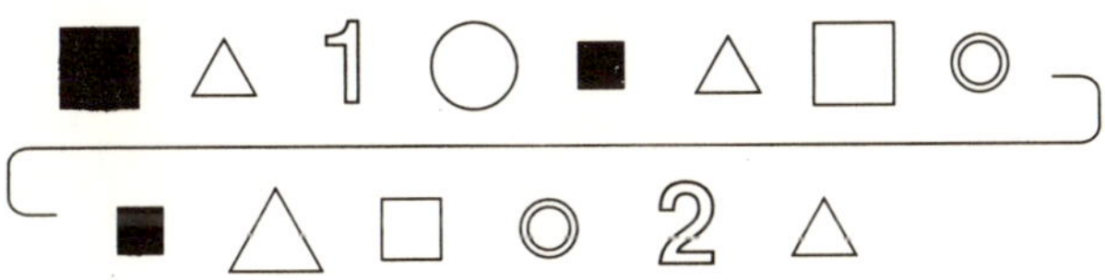

1 =

2 =

20.

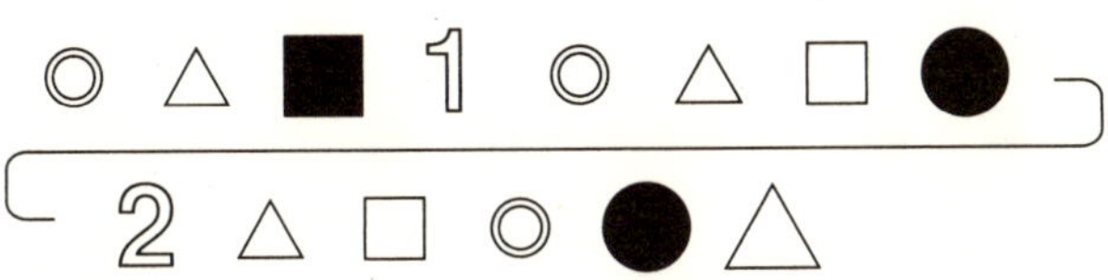

1 =

2 =

21.

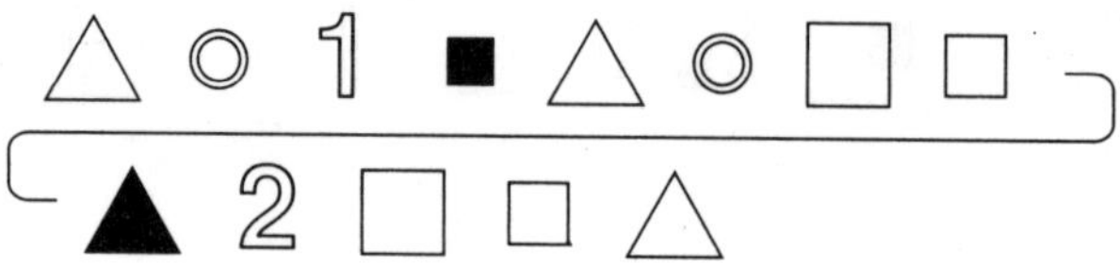

1 =
2 =

22.

1 =
2 =

23.

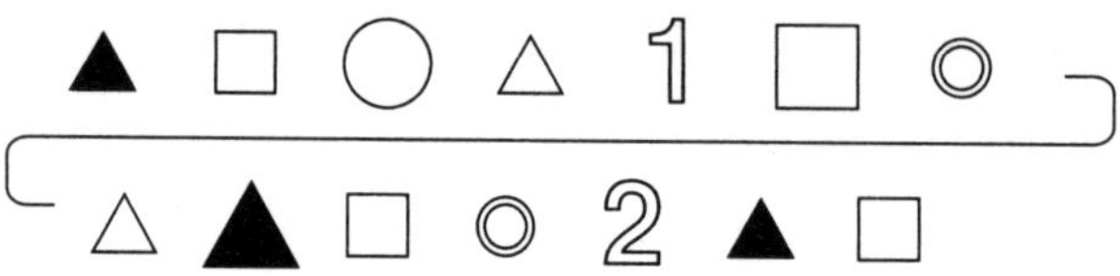

1 =
2 =

24.

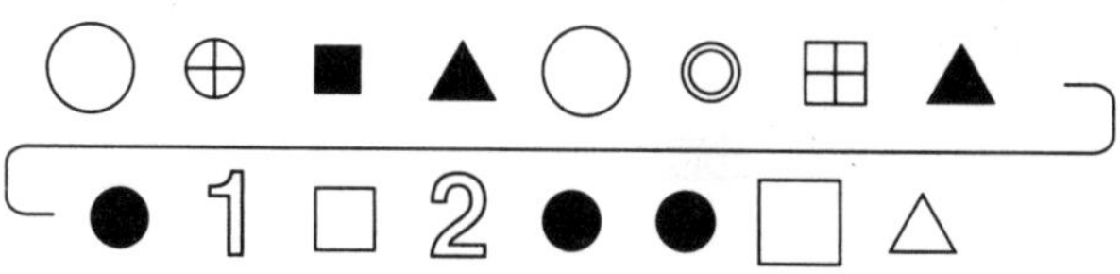

1 =
2 =

25.

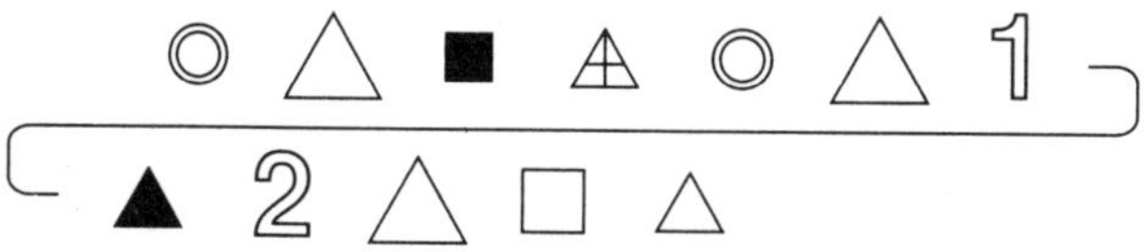

1 =
2 =

26.

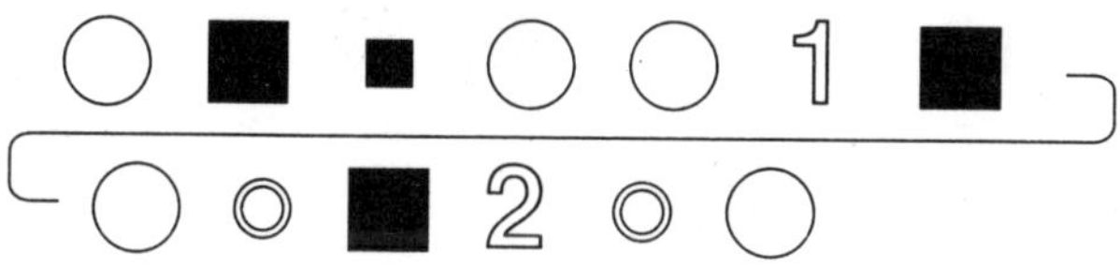

1 =
2 =

27.

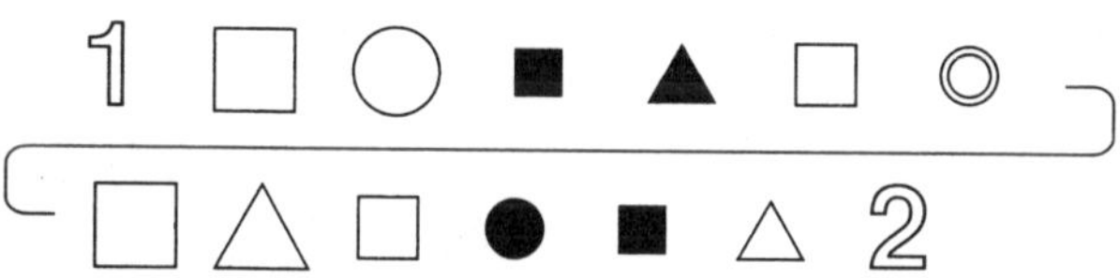

1 =
2 =

28.

1 =
2 =

29.

1 =
2 =

30.

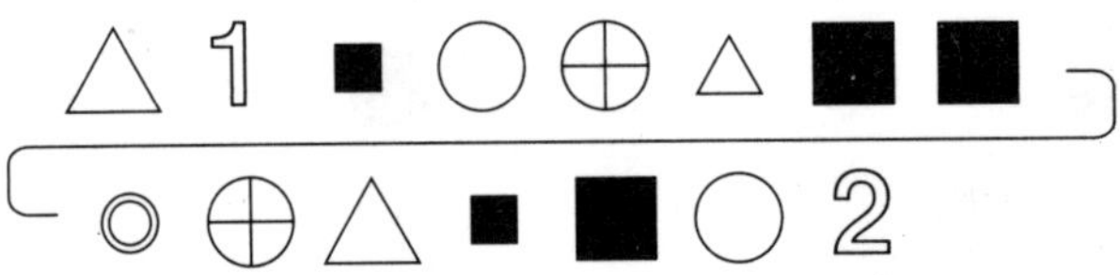

1 =
2 =

31.

1 =
2 =

32.

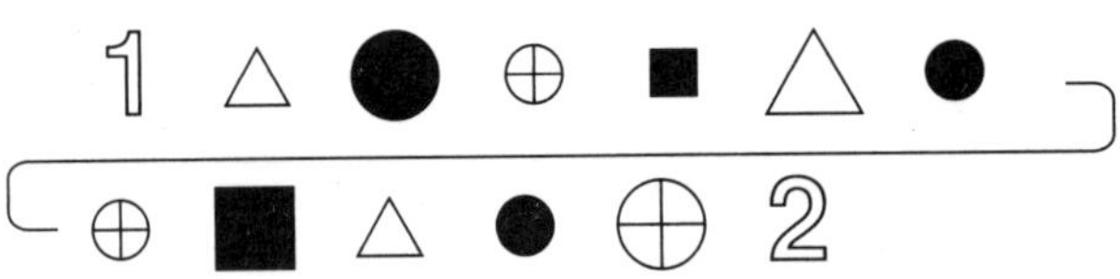

1 =
2 =

Answers

1. 1 = E, 2 = D	9. 1 = B, 2 = G	17. 1 = B, 2 = J	25. 1 = F, 2 = M
2. 1 = C, 2 = D	10. 1 = F, 2 = G	18. 1 = G, 2 = A	26. 1 = I, 2 = B
3. 1 = A, 2 = C	11. 1 = B, 2 = D	19. 1 = F, 2 = B	27. 1 = E, 2 = H
4. 1 = C, 2 = F	12. 1 = A, 2 = I	20. 1 = G, 2 = G	28. 1 = F, 2 = J
5. 1 = B, 2 = E	13. 1 = H, 2 = I	21. 1 = H, 2 = C	29. 1 = C, 2 = J
6. 1 = E, 2 = F	14. 1 = I, 2 = A	22. 1 = A, 2 = C	30. 1 = B, 2 = M
7. 1 = C, 2 = E	15. 1 = D, 2 = E	23. 1 = K, 2 = A	31. 1 = E, 2 = F
8. 1 = D, 2 = A	16. 1 = G, 2 = H	24. 1 = G, 2 = O	32. 1 = I, 2 = I

Scoring

Number right minus number wrong = ________

Plus 3 aged under 16, plus 1 if aged 17–20 + ________

Score on the test = ________

Use the following table to convert your test score to a score out of 10 or 'sten score'. You can then enter your 'sten score' in the chart on page 200.

Test score	1–2	3–5	6–8	9–10	11–12	13–14	15–18	19–21	22–24	25+
Sten score	1	2	3	4	5	6	7	8	9	10

Test 3

Perceptual

There are two types of problem in this test. In one type, you have to decide which of the objects is the 'odd one out'. In the second type you are shown a sequence of objects or shapes. Your task is to choose, from the alternatives you are given, the one that would come next in line.

Example 1

Which is the odd one out?

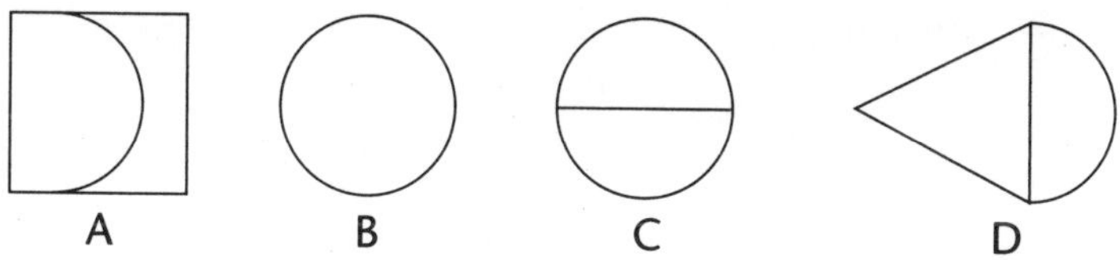

Example 2

Which comes next in the top line?

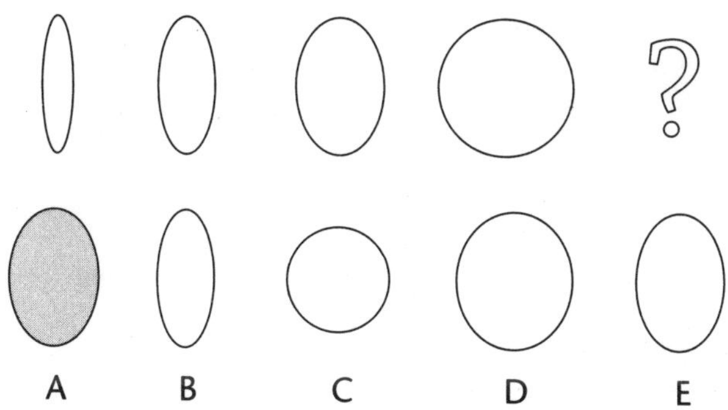

In Example 1, B is the correct answer. It is the only curved shape that does not also have a straight line.

In Example 2, the figures are of a circle that is turning. The figures can also be seen as a shape that is expanding by equal amounts until it becomes a full circle. The next step would be for the circle to turn by the same amount as before, or to decrease by the same amount as before. E is the correct answer. Although A is the correct shape, there is no reason why it should be shaded. D is not quite the correct size because it has not turned enough. B is not correct because it has turned too much. C is the wrong size and has not turned at all.

Do not mark this book if it is not your own, but record your answers and any working out you need to do on separate paper. If you wish to estimate your aptitude, record the number of the question you are on after exactly 10 minutes. Otherwise, take as long as you wish to complete the items.

Timed test: 10 minutes

1. Which is the odd one out?

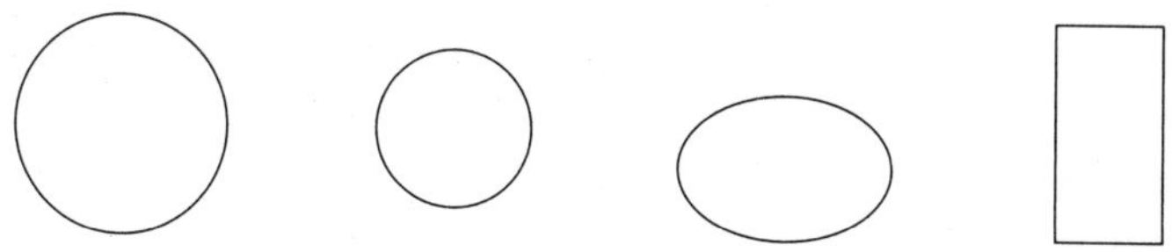

A B C D

2. Which comes next?

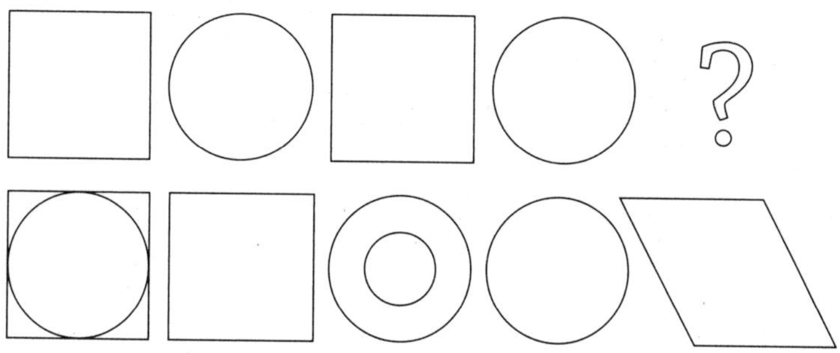

A B C D E

3. Which is the odd one out?

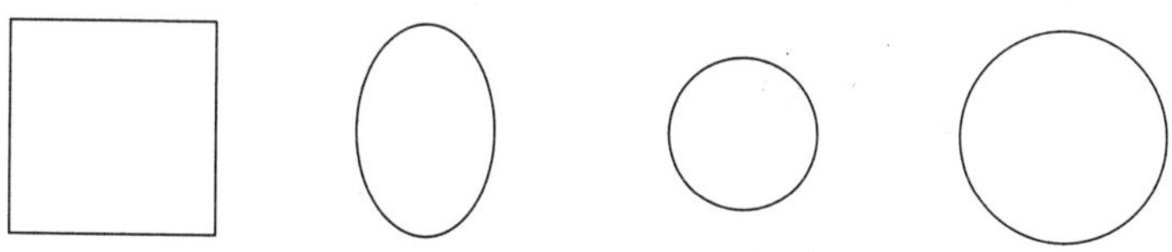

A B C D

4. Which comes next?

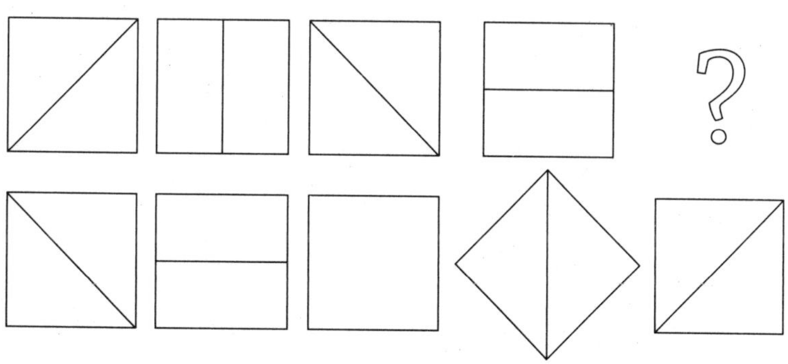

A B C D E

5. Which is the odd one out?

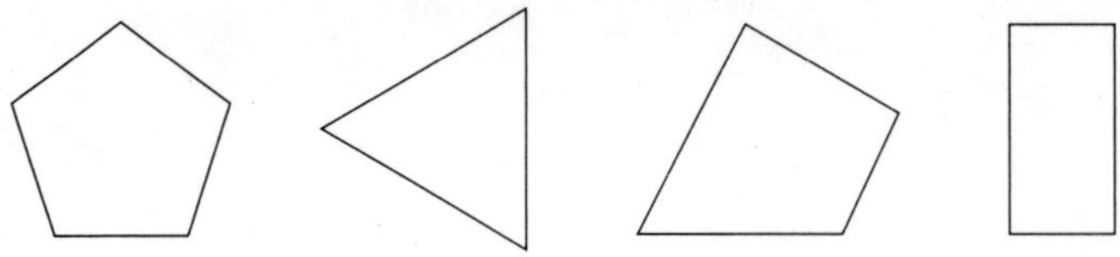

A B C D

6. Which comes next?

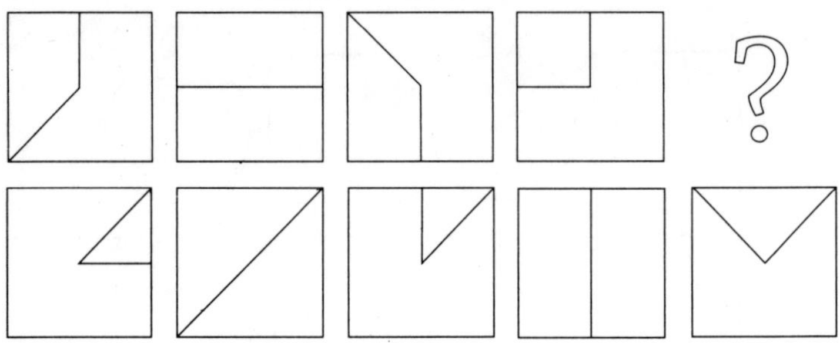

A B C D E

7. Which is the odd one out?

A B C D

8. Which comes next?

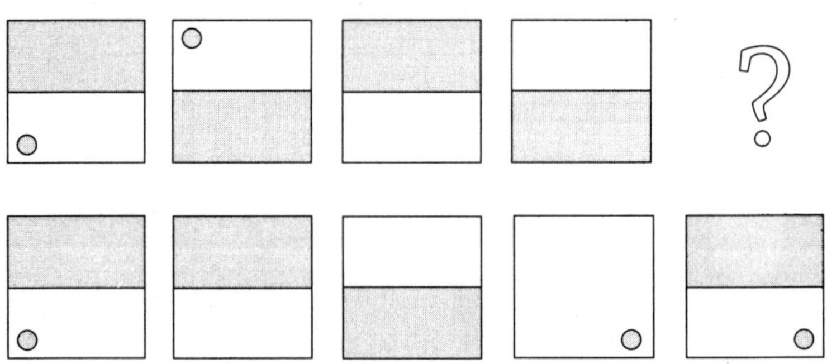

A B C D E

9. Which is the odd one out?

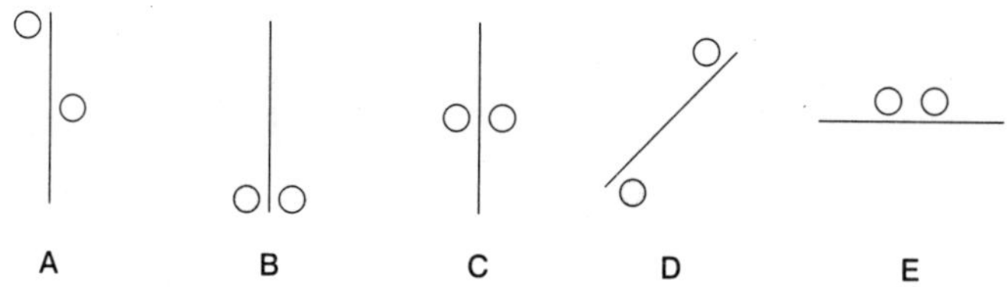

10. Which comes next?

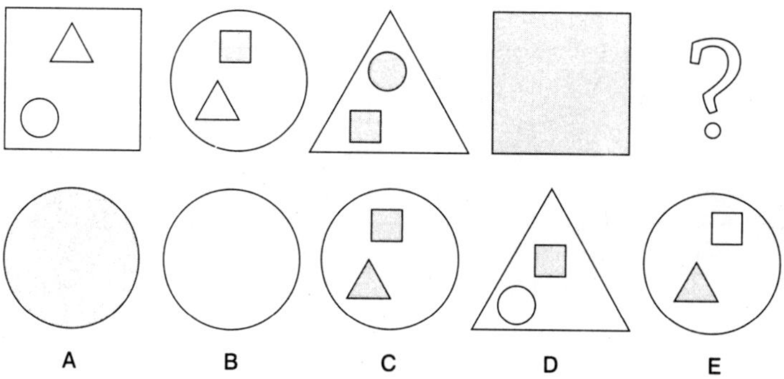

11. Which is the odd one out?

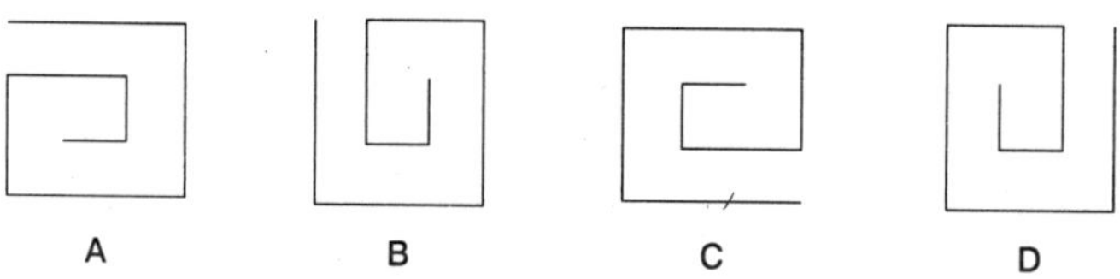

12. Which comes next?

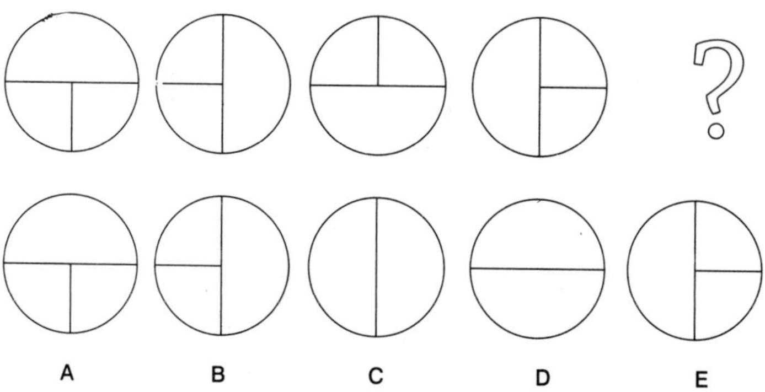

13. Which is the odd one out?

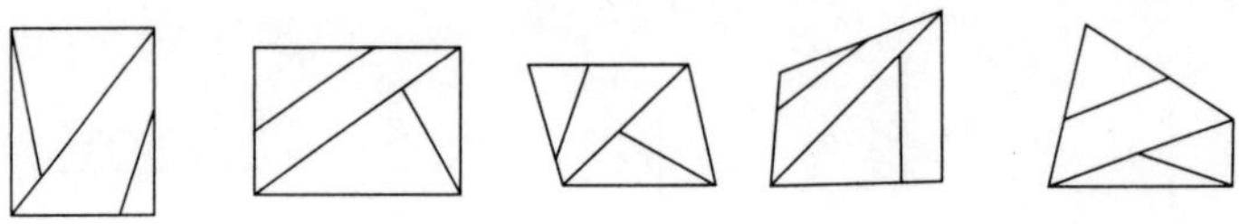

A B C D E

14. Which comes next?

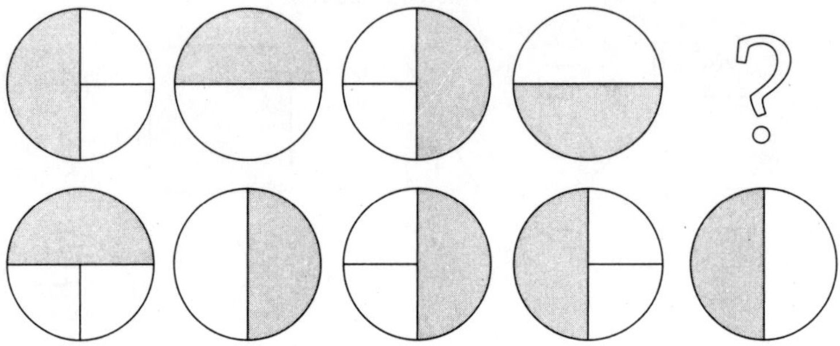

A B C D E

15. Which is the odd one out?

A B C D

16. Which comes next?

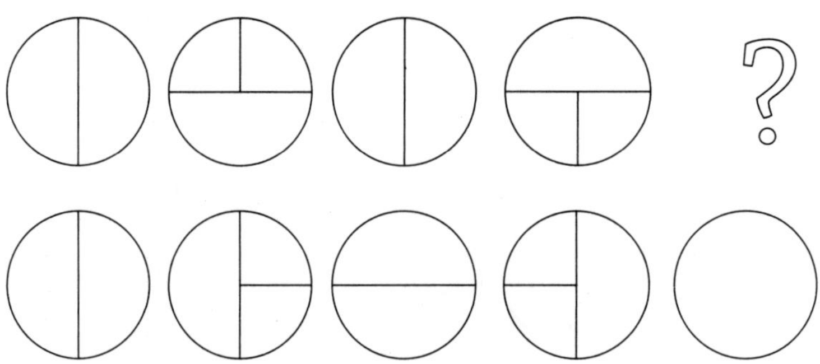

A B C D E

17. Which is the odd one out?

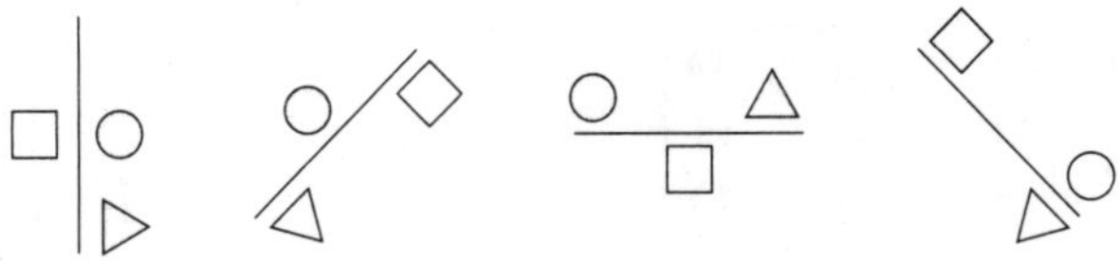

A B C D

18. Which comes next?

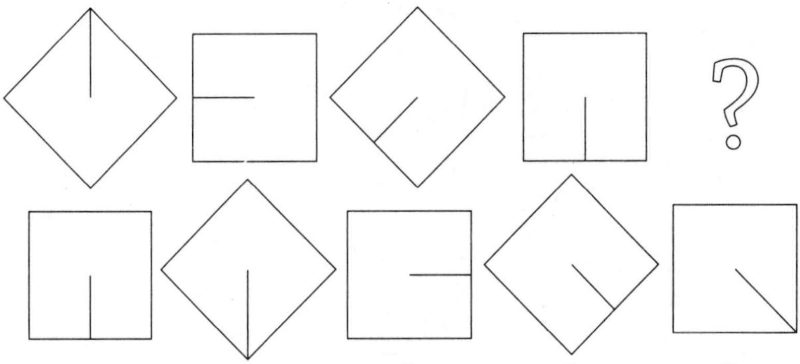

A B C D E

19. Which is the odd one out?

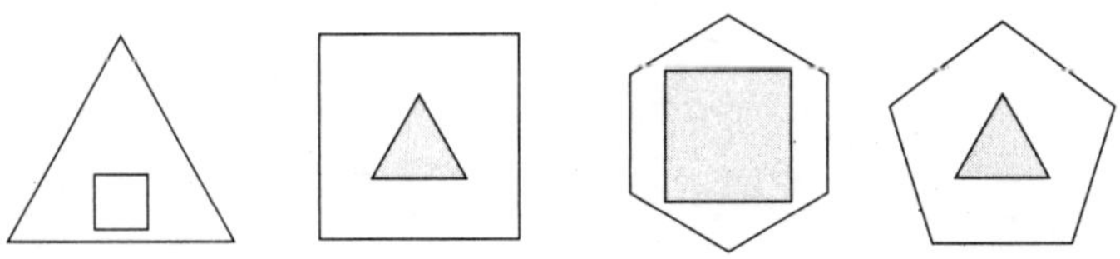

A B C D

20. Which comes next?

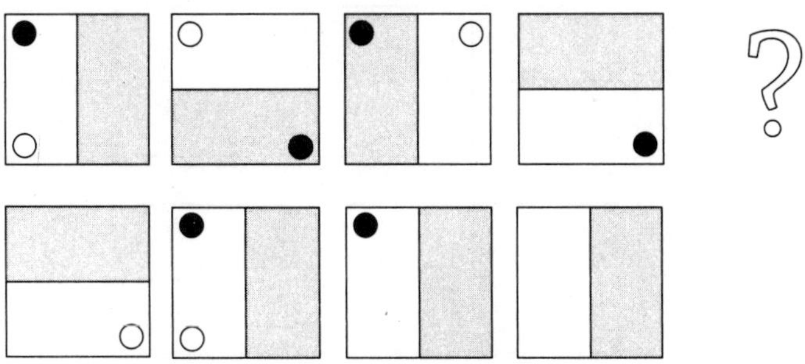

A B C D

21. Which is the odd one out?

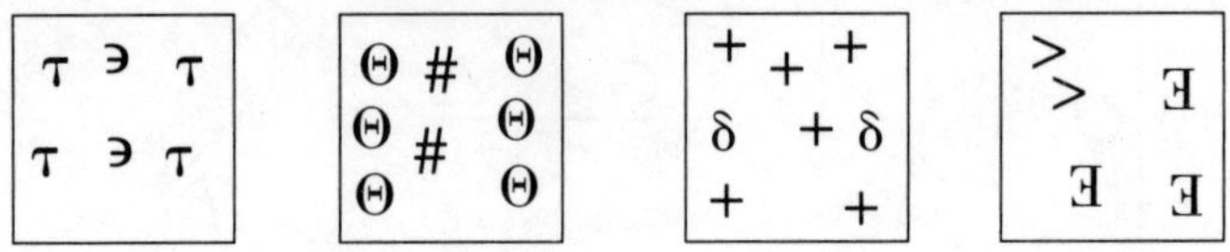

A B C D

22. Which comes next?

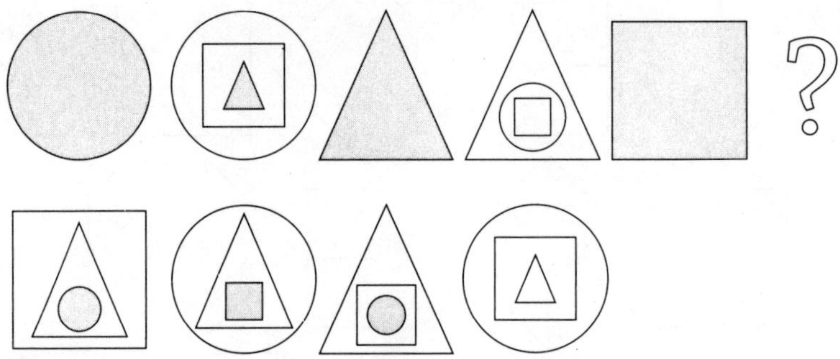

A B C D

23. Which is the odd one out?

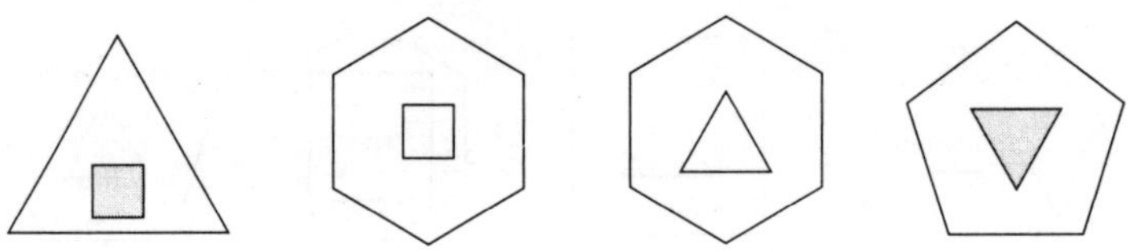

A B C D

24. Which comes next?

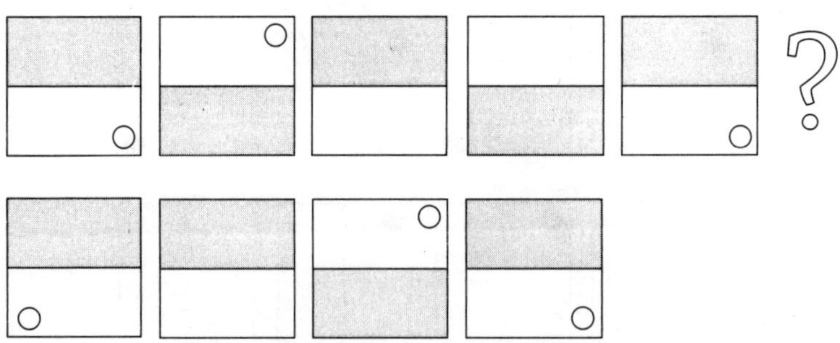

A B C D

25. Which is the odd one out?

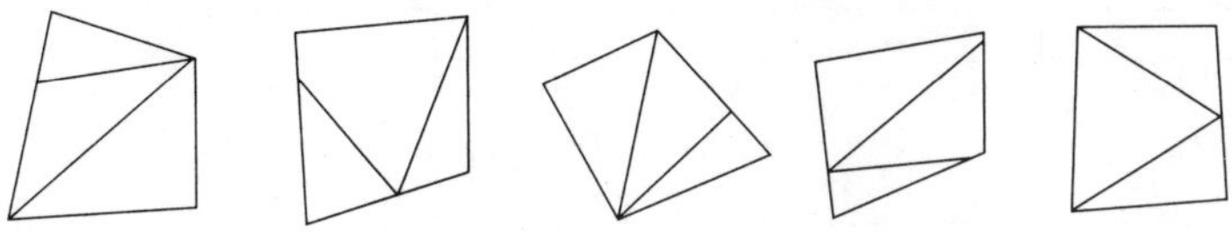

A B C D E

26. Which comes next?

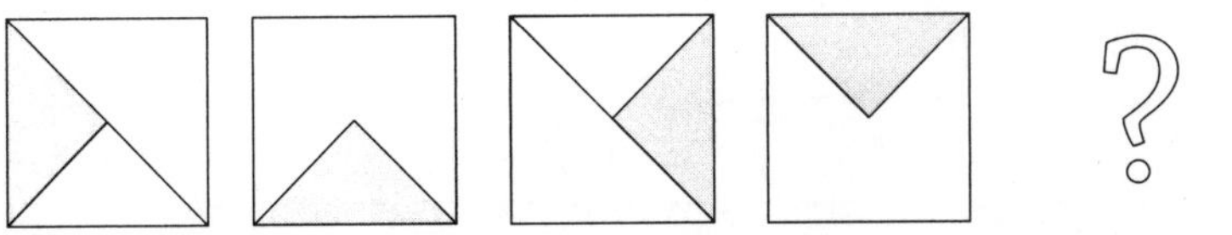

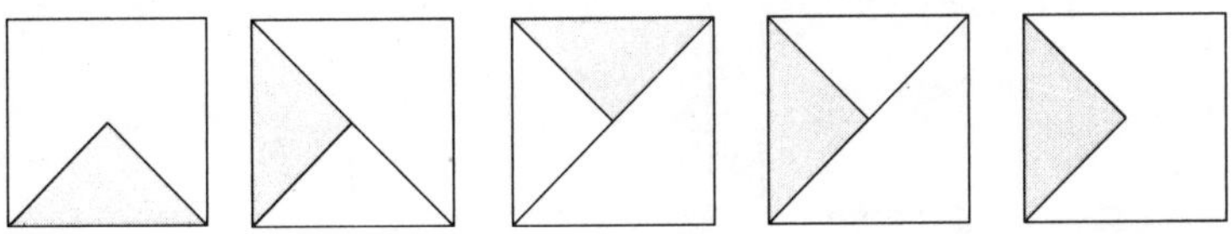

A B C D E

27. Which is the odd one out?

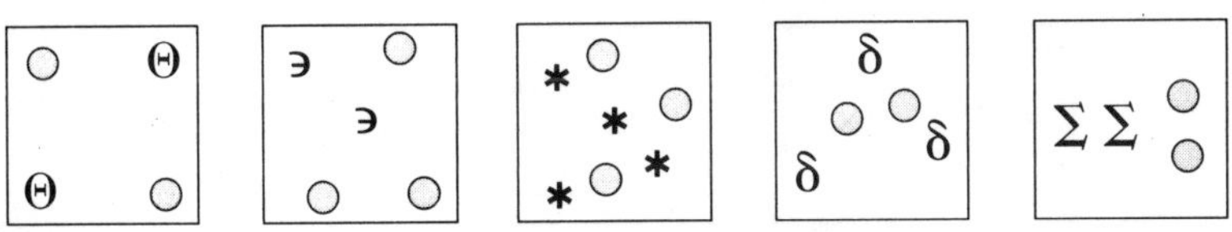

A B C D E

28. Which comes next?

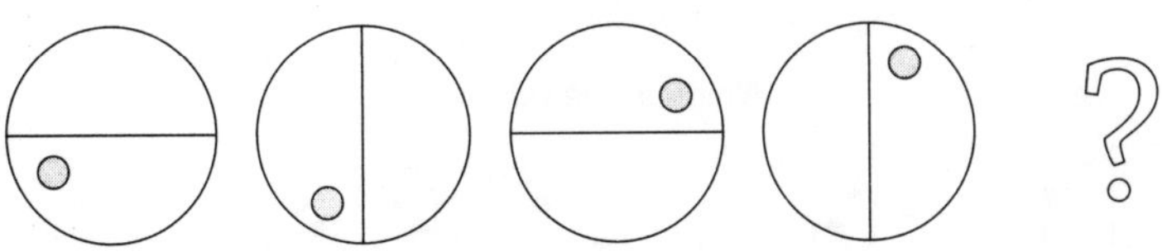

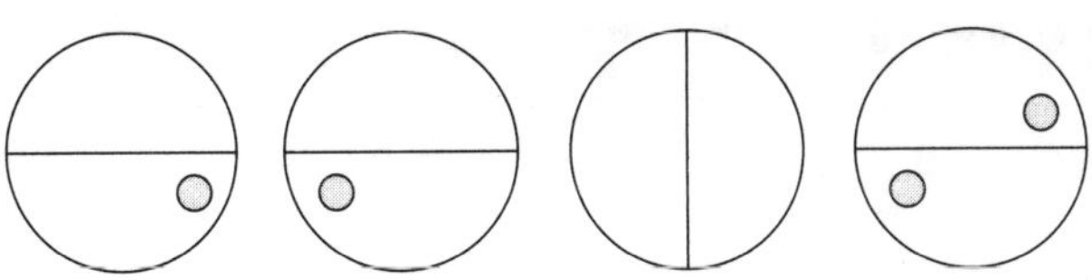

A B C D

29. Which is the odd one out?

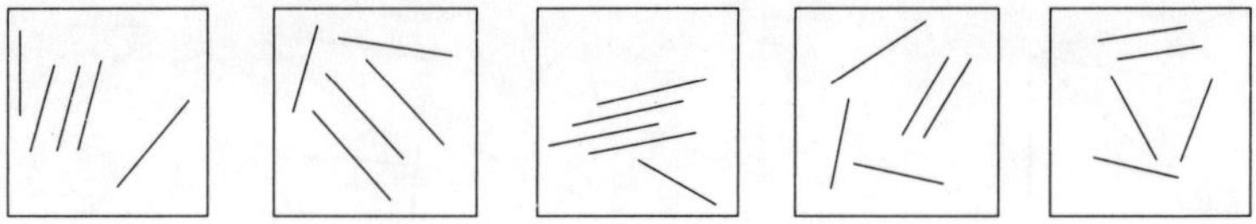

A B C D E

30. Which comes next?

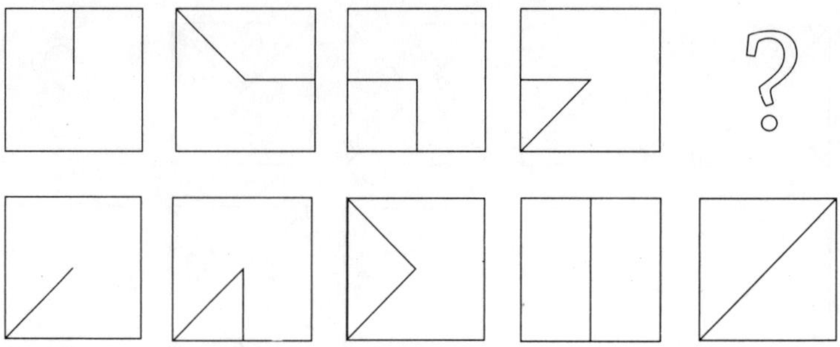

A B C D E

31. Which is the odd one out?

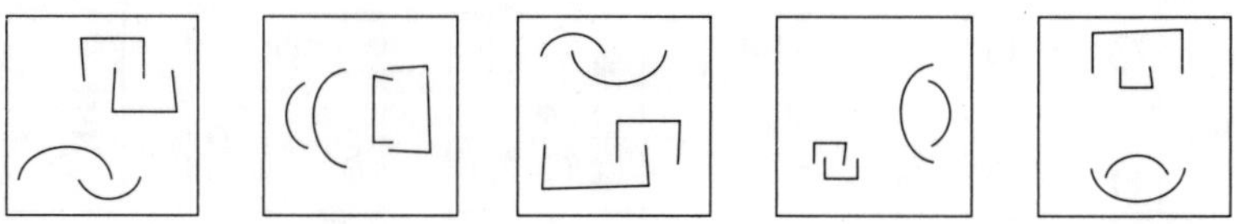

A B C D E

32. Which is the odd one out?

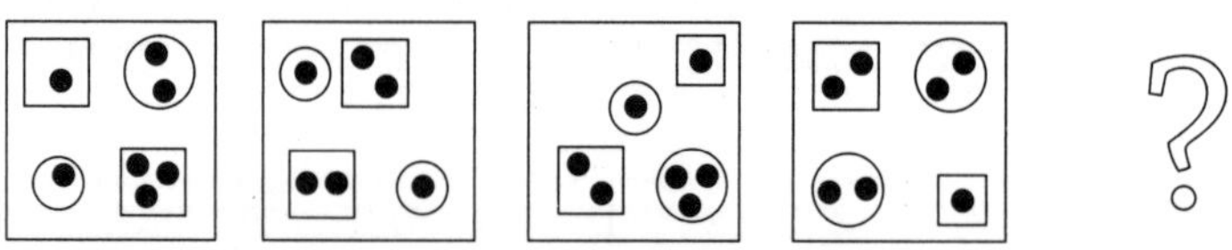

A B C D

Answers

1. D	9. E	17. D	25. E
2. B	10. A	18. D	26. B
3. A	11. B	19. A	27. B
4. E	12. A	20. B	28. B
5. C	13. D	21. B	29. C
6. C	14. D	22. A	30. D
7. C	15. C	23. A	31. D
8. A	16. A	24. C	32. B

Scoring

Number right minus number wrong = _________

Plus 3 aged under 16, plus 1 if aged 17–20 + _________

Score on the test = _________

Use the following table to convert your test score to a score out of 10 or 'sten score'. You can then enter your 'sten score' in the chart on page 200.

Test score	1–2	3–4	5–6	7–9	10–12	13–15	16–18	19–21	22–25	26+
Sten score	1	2	3	4	5	6	7	8	9	10

Part 2

Abstract numerical tests

You are not expected to be proficient with arithmetic or mathematics in either of these tests. The numbers are only used as a device in which relationships are formed. Whilst it is necessary to know the basic rules of numbers – addition, subtraction, multiplication and division – only a minimal ability with these is required to grasp the larger, conceptual issues of how the numbers relate to each other. The aptitude being tested is the ability to assess the proportions of things, make comparative judgements and see how matters 'shape up' when other proportions are added or substituted. The process of thinking requires a balance of quantification, proportion and adjustment, checking and proving possibilities. Doing well in these tests may indicate a high level of mathematical potential, which is especially relevant to careers where evaluation of data and the determination of their significance are important.

Test 4, Reasoning, asks that you discover identical information in a different form from which the original is presented. You have to identify the essential elements that may find a correspondence elsewhere, then test and prove your assumptions. Establishing what is relevant and what can be discarded can find expression in careers in which expert comprehension of quantitative issues is valued, for example, senior financial and economic roles.

Test 5, Interpolation, is a similar way of investigating abstract, numerical potential. But where, in Test 4, the problem has to be approached 'from all sides', the problems in Interpolation are more obviously logical and sequential. You have to consider the proportions and relationships that are holding the problem together or the missing elements that will make the equation balance. Again, the potential for mathematics is assessed and where the result is higher than for verbal tests it is likely that suitable careers would have a numerical basis.

Test 4

Reasoning

Find out whether a pair of numbers matches any of the possible answer pairs. One of the pairs *sometimes* has a relationship with *one* of the four possible answers a), b), c) or d). You have to find the answer that matches one of the pairs. When none of the pairs matches any of the answers, tick e).

Example 1

1:2

a) 1:1 b) 2:1 c) 3:2 d) 3:7 e) none

Explanation of Example 1: for the pair you are given, one number is half the other number: 1 is half of 2; 2 is two times 1. The same relationship is true for answer b). It does not matter that the numbers are the other way round.

For the next example, look at the first pair, 4:2, and see if there is a relationship with any of the possible answer pairs. If not, look at the next pair, 9:3, to see if that pair has a relationship with any of the answer pairs. Possibly, neither has a relationship with any of the given answer pairs, in which case your answer would be e).

Example 2

4:2 9:3

a) 1:4 b) 2:7 c) 3:2 d) 1:3 e) none

Explanation of Example 2: the correct answer is d) because 1:3 goes with 9:3. With each, the larger figure is *three times* the smaller figure. The fact that the numbers are around the other way does not matter. Sometimes the numbers are the same way, sometimes they are not, and sometimes there is no relationship at all. None of the other possible answers fits with the other pair.

Example 3

4:16

a) 2:1 b) 3:7 c) 1:2 d) 4:1 e) none

Example 4

3:12 9:3

a) 4:5 b) 1:7 c) 1:5 d) 6:4 e) none

The answer to Example 3 is d) because 4:1 is the same relationship as 4:16. The answer to Example 4 is e) because none of the possible answers has a relationship with either of the possible pairs.

The test begins on the next page. Work as quickly and accurately as you can. You can do the items in any order you like, although the questions get increasingly difficult. Do not mark this book if it is not your own, but record your answers and any working out you need to do on separate paper. If you wish to gain an estimate of your aptitude, record the number of the question you are on after exactly 10 minutes. Otherwise, take as long as you wish to complete the items.

Timed test: 10 minutes

1. **1:2**
a) 2:2 b) 6:1 c) 1:8 d) 1:2 e) none

2. **1.3**
a) 3:1 b) 1:6 c) 2:1 d) 5:4 e) none

3. **4:8**
a) 3:4 b) 8:4 c) 5:5 d) 3:3 e) none

4. **6:3**
a) 3:2 b) 4:9 c) 5:4 d) 2:2 e) none

5. **2:1**
a) 7:8 b) 1:1 c) 4:2 d) 6:5 e) none

6. **2:3**
a) 1:3 b) 7:1 c) 4:6 d) 9:3 e) none

7. **5:1**
a) 1:6 b) 1:10 c) 10:9 d) 15:3 e) none

8. **14:7**
a) 12:10 b) 2:14 c) 8:3 d) 3:9 e) none

9. **3:6 1:3**
a) 1:2 b) 4:1 c) 5:1 d) 3:3 e) none

10. **1:1 3:3**
a) 1:6 b) 3:4 c) 2:9 d) 4:4 e) none

11. **2:4 4:1**
a) 4:5 b) 3:3 c) 1:5 d) 7:3 e) none

12. **3:2 2:8**
a) 1:5 b) 4:1 c) 9:1 d) 1:11 e) none

13. **12:6 10:2**
a) 3:1 b) 5:1 c) 1:4 d) 4:1 e) none

14. **26:13 15.3**
a) 3:1 b) 1:6 c) 2:1 d) 5:4 e) none

15. **16:8 24:8**
a) 1:4 b) 3:4 c) 5:1 d) 1:3 e) none

16. **4:20 9.18 6:36**
a) 6:2 b) 4:5 c) 6:1 d) 2:20 e) none

17. **15:3 6:24 5:10**
a) 7:2 b) 3:1 c) 5:2 d) 6:1 e) none

18. **100:50 27:9 32:8**
a) 10:3 b) 5:1 c) 2:16 d) 9:3 e) none

19. **12:2 13:2 4:8**
a) 1:6 b) 1:4 c) 2:2 d) 1:3 e) none

20. **24:3 15:6 4:28**
a) 12:2 b) 14:2 c) 8:3 d) 3:10 e) none

21. **3:4 9:3 1:3 8:4**
a) 1:2 b) 1:4 c) 1:5 d) 6:10 e) none

22. **9:3 5:23 4:21 2:24**
a) 1:4 b) 5:3 c) 12:9 d) 12:2 e) none

23. **9:5 6:4 13:8 15:9**
a) 4:2 b) 3:1 c) 1:4 d) 3:7 e) none

24. **6:20 30:7 23:3 22:2**
a) 5:1 b) 1:4 c) 5:1 d) 3:33 e) none

25. **15:9 24:20 7:35 11:10**
a) 12:4 b) 8:64 c) 10:2 d) 1:1 e) none

26. **100:10 11:111 7:70 35:7**
a) 1:11 b) 5:1 c) 7:1 d) 10:11 e) none

27. **4:6 9:5 14:2 16:14**
a) 7:8 b) 12:6 c) 1:2 d) 7:6 e) none

28. **16:3 24:5 44:10 36:3**
a) 5:12 b) 11:4 c) 5:1 d) 12:1 e) none

29. **100:11 8:88 27:3 128:16**
a) 8:1 b) 10:1 c) 22:1 d) 32:2 e) none

30. **51:6 126:18 38:3 28:4**
a) 14.1 b) 24:8 c) 15:3 d) 17:2 e) none

31. **14:3 19:6 11:32 17:26**
a) 6:3 b) 7:3 c) 7:2 d) 3:4 e) none

32. **13:12 10:9 9:8 8:11**
a) 96:104 b) 60:52 c) 128:256 d) 48:45 e) none

33. **3:5 4:3 7:4 9:5**
a) 54:48 b) 16:20 c) 66:44 d) 28:16 e) none

34. **512:128 444:333 99:297 153:68**
a) 12:20 b) 63:21 c) 8:13 d) 17:11 e) none

35. **13:11 39:55 66:26 52:99 165:110**
a) 54:26 b) 14:4 c) 16:24 d) 15:12 e) none

36. **17:8 19:13 21:20 39:43 29:19**
a) 88:178 b) 4:7 c) 48:95 d) 95:145 e) none

Answers

1. d	7. d	13. b	19. a	25. c	31. e
2. a	8. e	14. c	20. b	26. b	32. a
3. b	9. a	15. d	21. a	27. a	33. d
4. e	10. d	16. c	22. e	28. d	34. b
5. c	11. e	17. e	23. e	29. a	35. c
6. c	12. b	18. d	24. d	30. d	36. d

Scoring

Number right minus number wrong = __________

Plus 3 aged under 16, plus 1 if aged 17–20 + __________

Score on the test = __________

Use the following table to convert your test score to a score out of 10 or 'sten score'. You can then enter your 'sten score' in the chart on page 200.

Test score	1–5	6–9	10–13	14–17	18–20	21–23	24–26	27–28	29–30	31+
Sten score	1	2	3	4	5	6	7	8	9	10

Test 5

Interpolation

In this test you are given numbers that connect in some way. They connect along the row, but there is also a relationship with the numbers that are above or below each other. Sometimes a number is missing and a space mark, or line (–) has been put in its place. One of the numbers has been replaced by a question mark (?).

From the information given, you have to find the number that would replace the question mark.

Example 1

1	–	3	?	
–	4	6	8	Answer = ☐

The most logical answer is 4, because it fits the sequence 1, 2, 3, 4 as a 2 could replace the space mark. Also, 4 is half of 8, in the same way that 3 is half of 6, 2 is half of 4, and 1 is half of 2. The answer, 4, makes all the numbers fit together logically:

1	2	3	4	
2	4	6	8	Answer = ☐

Example 2

1	–	9	?	
2	6	–	54	Answer = ☐

The numbers in the lower line are always twice the number in the row above. Also, from left to right, each number is multiplied three times.

1	3	9	27	
2	6	18	54	Answer = ☐

Working out the correct numbers for the empty spaces can help you find the number that can replace the question mark. The test begins on the next page. Work as quickly and accurately as you can. You can do the items in any order you like, although the questions get increasingly difficult. Do not mark this book if it is not your own, but record your answers and any working out you need to do on separate paper. If you wish to gain an estimate of your aptitude, record the number of the question you are on after exactly 8 minutes. Otherwise, take as long as you wish to complete the items.

Timed test: 8 minutes

1.

4	3	2	?
4	–	2	1

Answer = ☐

2.

2	4	6	–
4	?	12	16

Answer = ☐

3.

1	?	5	7	–
–	6	–	–	18

Answer = ☐

4.

–	–	8	4	?
64	32	–	–	4

Answer = ☐

5.

2	3	?	–	12
–	–	5	8	12

Answer = ☐

6.

3	6	9	12
9	?	–	36

Answer = ☐

7.

25	16	9	4
–	4	?	2

Answer = ☐

8.

3	7	?	–
4	8	16	32

Answer = ☐

9.

7	12	22	–	82
–	4	9	19	?

Answer = ☐

10.

13	14	16	?	28
1	–	4	–	8

Answer = ☐

11.

3	7	16	35	?
1	2	3	–	5

Answer = ☐

12.

11	14	–	?
33	42	60	87

Answer = ☐

13.

3	6	5	8	7	–
7	11	11	15	15	?

Answer = ☐

14.	?	5	7	12	–		
	3	–	8	13	21		Answer =

15.	4	5	8	10	?	20	
	10	8	20	16	40	–	Answer =

16.	3	7	5	?	7	11	
	–	4	2	4	2	–	Answer =

17.	5	10	7	12	–		
	10	30	?	60	54		Answer =

18.	6	13	20	–	34		
	?	24	37	–	63		Answer =

19.	0	5	3	13	11	?	
	5	–	10	2	20	–	Answer =

20.	13	?	22	31	53		
	78	45	–	93	–		Answer =

Answers

1. 1	6. 18	11. 74	16. 9
2. 8	7. 3	12. 29	17. 28
3. 3	8. 15	13. 19	18. 11
4. 2	9. 39	14. 2	19. 31
5. 5	10. 20	15. 16	20. 9

Scoring

Number right minus number wrong = __________

Plus 2 aged under 16, plus 1 if aged 17–20 + __________

Score on the test = __________

Use the following table to convert your test score to a score out of 10 or 'sten score'. You can then enter your 'sten score' in the chart on page 200.

Test score	1–2	3	4–5	6	7–8	9	10–12	13	14–15	16+
Sten score	1	2	3	4	5	6	7	8	9	10

Part 3

Abstract verbal tests

In the same way that the abstract numerical tests require some ability to count and to understand the rules of numbers, the abstract verbal tests require an understanding of what words mean and how sentences are formed to convey meaning. The vocabulary is not difficult, but forming accurate conclusions about what is being communicated becomes increasingly difficult as the tests proceed. The skill required lies in being able to evaluate information without being distracted by false information and without making assumptions about something that is not actually there. This type of verbal test is more likely to be confusing than any other type of test simply because words can have several meanings and all of us are sometimes taken in by distorted messages as well as those deliberately intended to deceive.

Tests 6 and 7 have a similar layout and are measuring essentially the same deductive potential. Be especially aware of the necessity of making logical conclusions from information that is given to you in an 'oblique way', that is in a way that can be derived from other clues. Success on this test really does require a kind of aptitude that has much in common with detection. Test 6, Deduction, is a 'real' test that has been used by organizations to help discover executives with high-level reasoning skills. It is also very similar to the type of problems given to applicants for senior positions in public administration and for entry to business schools. Test 7, Analysis, is similarly demanding, but has been designed to be taken by younger people who may still be at school as well as by older people.

Success on these tests is a good indicator of 'academic' potential, particularly if you are good on the abstract numerical tests too. People who do well on these tests are generally good communicators in management or in other direct, face-to-face situations.

Test 6

Deduction

In this test you have to find the conclusion that follows from the information you are given. Sometimes there is information missing, but you will have enough to form a correct answer.

Read through the example below, which has been done for you. Before looking at the answers, try to work them out for yourself, ticking the answer to each question you think is correct. You will probably find it useful to have scrap paper available.

Example

Whilst Mr Black, Mr Saul and Mr Hardy travel to work by bus, Mr Jones and Mr Peters travel by train. Mr Black and Mr Saul also walk part of the way. Mr Saul, Mr Peters and Mr Hardy have season tickets.

1) Who has a season ticket, but also walks?

a) Mr Black b) Mr Saul c) Mr Hardy
d) Mr Jones e) Mr Peters f) cannot say

2) Who does not have a season ticket and does not walk?

a) Mr Black b) Mr Saul c) Mr Hardy
d) Mr Jones e) Mr Peters f) cannot say

3) Who travels by bus, but does not have a season ticket?

a) Mr Black b) Mr Saul c) Mr Hardy
d) Mr Jones e) Mr Peters f) cannot say

4) How many people have neither a season ticket nor walk?

a) Mr Black b) Mr Saul c) Mr Hardy
d) Mr Jones e) Mr Peters f) cannot say

5) Who lives closest to a bus stop?

a) Mr Black b) Mr Saul c) Mr Hardy
d) Mr Jones e) Mr Peters f) cannot say

The answers are: 1) b, Mr Saul; 2) d, Mr Jones; 3) a, Mr Black; 4) a, one; 5) f, cannot say.

With problems of this type, it can be useful to lay out the information provided in the form of a table or diagram. This means that you do not have to 'carry' all the information in your head. Have spare paper available. The following is a possible way of laying out the information in the example problem:

Black	*Saul*	*Hardy*	*Jones*	*Peters*
bus	bus	bus	train	train
walk	walk			
	season	season		season

On the next page are several sets of information and you have to tick the correct answers. You can do the items in any order you like, although the questions get increasingly difficult. Do not mark this book if it is not your own, but record your answers and any working out you need to do on separate paper. If you wish to gain an estimate of your aptitude, record the number of the question you are on after exactly 20 minutes. Otherwise, take as long as you wish to complete the items.

Timed test: 20 minutes

A. Of three part-time employees, Mary Potter works longer hours than Fred Ruby, although Betty Simpson works longer hours than Mary Potter.

1. Who works the longest hours?

a) Mary Potter b) Fred Ruby c) Betty Simpson
d) cannot say

B. Frank and John use computers in their work. Gary, John and Frank are self-employed. Frank and Jack work part-time, whilst the others are all full-time. Jack and John are the only ones who work in insurance.

2. Who uses a computer to work full-time in insurance?

a) Frank b) John c) Jack
d) Gary e) cannot say

3. Who does not work in insurance and does not have a computer?

a) Frank b) John c) Jack
d) Gary e) cannot say

4. Who is the only one who is self-employed and works part-time?

a) Frank b) John c) Jack
d) Gary e) cannot say

C. Different businesses occupy a three-storey building. The Architect is on the top floor, whilst the Estate Agent is on the floor below the Travel Agent. The Accountant is on the floor above the Publisher, as is the Estate Agent. The Travel Agent is on the same floor as the Car Rental Company. On the floor between the Publisher and the Car Rental Company is a Detective Agency.

5. Which business is on a floor by itself?

a) Architect b) Estate Agent c) Travel Agent
d) Accountant e) Publisher f) Car Rental
g) Detective h) cannot say

6. Which business occupies the largest floor space?

a) Architect b) Estate Agent c) Travel Agent
d) Accountant e) Publisher f) Car Rental
g) Detective h) cannot say

7. Of the options given, which business is on the same floor as the Accountant?

a) Architect b) Estate Agent c) Travel Agent
d) Accountant e) Publisher f) Car Rental
g) Detective h) cannot say

D. Sally, Cheryl, Laura, Tom and Sandy travel extensively on business. Four of them have visas for China. All, apart from Cheryl and Tom, have visas for Russia. Cheryl's only visa is for Pakistan, although only Sally and Sandy do not have a visa for Pakistan.

8. Who only has visas for China and Pakistan?

a) Sally b) Cheryl c) Laura
d) Tom e) Sandy f) cannot say

9. Who has the most visas?

a) Sally b) Cheryl c) Laura
d) Tom e) Sandy f) cannot say

10. Who travels most often?

a) Sally b) Cheryl c) Laura
d) Tom e) Sandy f) cannot say

11. Who are the two people who have identical visas?

a) Sally b) Cheryl c) Laura
d) Tom e) Sandy f) cannot say

12. How many visas do the group have between them?

a) 4 b) 5 c) 6
d) 7 e) 8 f) 9
g) 10 h) 11 i) 12
j) 13 k) 14 l) 15
m) 16 n) 17

13. Which is the most frequented country?

a) Pakistan b) Russia c) China
d) cannot say

E. Three athletes each receive a first, second and third prize for a different sporting event. Either Anne or Josie got the second prize for Tennis. Anne got the same prize for throwing the javelin as Josie got for swimming. Tanya got the first prize for swimming, and her prize for the javelin was the same as Josie's for tennis and Anne's for swimming.

14. Who got the first prize for tennis?

a) Anne b) Josie c) Tanya
d) cannot say

15. Who was best with the javelin?

a) Anne b) Josie c) Tanya
d) cannot say

16. Who got the second prize for swimming?

a) Anne b) Josie c) Tanya
d) cannot say

F. Doppler's butterfly is only found in Asian countries, including India, Thailand, Japan, Malaysia and Cambodia, and in areas of non-forested South American countries, including Brazil, Argentina, Chile and Peru. It is very rare in Brazil, where it has black, elongated wings, whilst in Asia the wings are much shorter and coloured orange. In Chile they have only red wings, though these retain the characteristic South American shape.

17. In which country is the butterfly unlikely to have elongated wings?

a) Mexico b) Chile c) Argentina
d) Brazil e) India f) cannot say

18. Where is a forest-dwelling Doppler butterfly with orange wings most likely to be found?

a) Chile b) Germany c) Thailand
d) Australia e) cannot say

19. Where is a desert-dwelling, elongated winged Doppler butterfly most likely to be found?

a) Thailand b) India c) Japan
d) Australia e) Argentina f) cannot say

20. Where is a purple Doppler butterfly most likely to be found?

a) France b) India c) Japan
d) Cambodia e) Peru f) cannot say

G. To get to his home at Tranton Park, Geoff takes the 17.45 train from Central Station. Rona avoids public transport whenever possible, but walks with him to the station, where she has left her car. Her drive to her home in Hampton takes 15 minutes, although it would have taken exactly the same time by train. Like Geoff, Sam takes the train, but avoids the rush by taking the 17.15 from Central Station. Bella, who works in the same office as the rest and who prefers the train, always makes the journey with Sam as far as Hampton, where she lives. Sam continues to Nately, which is his home town, a journey that is three times as long as hers. Geoff arrives at Tranton Park an hour and a quarter after Bella gets to Hampton.

21. Who probably has the longest journey?

a) Geoff b) Rona c) Sam
d) Bella e) cannot say

22. Who is most likely to arrive home first?

a) Geoff b) Rona c) Sam
d) Bella e) cannot say

23. Who, apart from Geoff, is most likely to travel by train?

a) Geoff b) Rona c) Sam
d) Bella e) cannot say

24. Who never travels by train?

a) Geoff b) Rona c) Sam
d) Bella e) cannot say

25. How many minutes is the journey time between Nately and Tranton Park?

a) 30 b) 15 c) 20
d) 10 e) 5 f) 45
g) cannot say

Answers

1. c	6. h	11. a/e	16. a	21. a
2. b	7. b/g	12. g	17. e	22. d
3. d	8. d	13. d	18. c	23. d
4. a	9. c	14. a	19. e	24. e
5. e	10. f	15. b	20. f	25. b

Scoring

Number right minus number wrong = ________

Plus 2 aged under 16, plus 1 if aged 17–20 + ________

Score on the test = ________

Use the following table to convert your test score to a score out of 10 or 'sten score'. You can then enter your 'sten score' in the chart on page 200.

Test score	1–6	7–8	9–10	11–12	13–14	15–16	17	18	19	20+
Sten score	1	2	3	4	5	6	7	8	9	10

Test 7

Analysis

This test looks at how well you can draw logical conclusions from the information you have been given. There is always sufficient information for you to work out the correct answer. You should not draw upon any previous experience or information you suppose might be relevant. You are given some facts and some possible answers. Tick the letter which corresponds with the correct answer.

Example 1

The town of Newport is further west than the town of Flatpeak, although not so far west as the town of Daybridge.

Which town is furthest east?
Answers: a) Newport b) Daybridge c) Flatpeak

The answer cannot be a) because Newport is west of Flatpeak. It cannot be b) because Daybridge is even further west, so Flatpeak must be to the east of Daybridge. The answer is c).

Example 2

Fred, Mack and John all have two different cars each. One of them does not have a Ford. Mack is the only one to have a Ferrari. John has a Ford. Fred and Mack have Buicks.

Who has a Rolls-Royce?
Answers: a) Fred b) Mack c) John

The answer is c). It cannot be a), because Fred has a Ford and a Buick. It cannot be b), because Mack has a Ferrari and a Buick.

Because of the amount of information you are sometimes asked to deal with, it is recommended that you have a piece of scrap paper so that you can, if you wish, make notes or plans. Tables like the following are often helpful.

		PEOPLE	
CARS	Fred	Mack	John
Ferrari			
Ford			
Buick			
Rolls-Royce			

You should have scrap paper and pencil ready in case you need them. Do not mark this book if it is not your own, but record your answers and any working out you need to do on separate paper. If you wish to gain an estimate of your aptitude, record the number of the question you are on after exactly 15 minutes. Otherwise, take as long as you wish to complete the items.

Timed test: 15 minutes

A. Emma lives further up the hill than Jane. Pauline lives further up the hill than Emma.

1. Who lives furthest up the hill?

   a) Emma b) Jane c) Pauline

B. All the girls like sport. Sue and Josie like Tennis, while Sally and Anne like Running. Both Sue and Anne like Swimming.

2. Who likes Tennis and Swimming?

   a) Sue b) Josie c) Sally d) Anne

3. Who likes Swimming and Running?

   a) Sue b) Josie c) Sally d) Anne

C. Mr Everton and Mr Soames have longer holidays that Mr Francke. Mr Porter has a shorter holiday than Mr Francke, whilst Mr Peters has a longer holiday than Mr Francke.

4. Who has the shortest holiday?

   a) Mr Everton b) Mr Soames c) Mr Francke
   d) Mr Porter e) Mr Peters

D. Toby, Rob and Frank all take a holiday by the sea, whilst Sam, Jo and Tony go hiking in the mountains. Frank, Sam and Jo travel by air. Jo, Rob and Tony do not enjoy their holiday.

5. Who goes to the sea and does not enjoy the holiday?

   a) Toby b) Rob c) Frank
   d) Sam e) Jo f) Tony

6. Who does not travel by air and goes hiking?

   a) Toby b) Rob c) Frank
   d) Sam e) Jo f) Tony

E. In reverse order, the most popular holiday tours offered by a travel company are Toronto, Florida, Rome and Paris, although Rome is extremely popular whatever the time of year. After a marketing promotion, Toronto becomes more popular than Rome, but less popular than Florida.

7. Which tour is most popular after the marketing promotion?

   a) Toronto b) Florida c) Rome d) Paris

8. Which tour is least popular after the marketing promotion?

   a) Toronto b) Rome c) Florida d) Paris

F. Fred, John, Garth and Joe all have children. Fred and John are the only two to have boys. John and Joe take their children to school by bus, whilst it is near enough to school for the others to walk. Fred and Joe are car owners, and sometimes do use their cars to get the children to school.

9. Who owns a car, but usually goes to work by bus?

   a) Fred b) Joe c) John d) Garth

10. Who does not own a car and has a daughter?

    a) Fred b) Joe c) John d) Garth

G. In a museum, Modern Sculpture is to be found on the floor below Watercolours. Greek Pottery is on the floor above the Oil Paintings. The top floor contains the Italian Collection. Watercolours are on the same floor as South American Art, whereas the Oil Paintings are on the floor below Modern Sculpture.

11. What is to be found on the lowest floor?

    a) Modern Sculpture b) Watercolours c) Greek Pottery
    d) Oil Paintings e) Italian Collection f) South American Art

12. Which two are on the same floor?

    a) Modern Sculpture and Greek Pottery
    b) Watercolours and Oil Paintings
    c) Oil Paintings and South American Art
    d) none of these

H. Casey, Stuart, Ritchie, Billie and Colin all buy their own vehicles. Casey and Colin have room for three passengers as well as themselves. The others only have room for one passenger besides themselves. Ritchie and Casey have good front tyres, though the other tyres on all of the other vehicles are dangerous. Casey and Billie have vehicles that use diesel fuel. The others have vehicles that use petrol.

13. Who can take three passengers in their diesel vehicle?

a) Casey b) Stuart c) Ritchie
d) Billie e) Colin

14. How many people have dangerous tyres on diesel vehicles that only have room for one passenger?

a) 5 b) 4 c) 3
d) 2 e) 1 f) none

15. Who can only take one passenger, but has good tyres?

a) Casey b) Stuart c) Ritchie
d) Billie e) Colin

I. Mrs Booth has difficulty feeding her four children as each one will only eat certain foods. Sharon and Robina will eat rice and lamb. Kelly and Sharon are the only ones who like bread and cheese. Kelly and Sam both eat chicken and bread.

16. Which is the only food that Sharon does not eat?

a) bread b) chicken c) lamb
d) rice e) cheese

17. Who eats cheese, chicken and bread?

a) Sharon b) Kelly c) Robina
d) Sam

18. Who does not eat cheese, but does eat lamb and rice?

a) Sharon b) Kelly c) Robina
d) Sam

19. Which food will be acceptable to most of the children?

a) bread b) rice c) lamb
d) cheese e) pasta

J. Mr Marx's and Mr Bagshaw's cars are black. The others have red ones. Mr Bagshaw and Mrs Chance have a white stripe on the sides of their cars. Miss Jenkins has a blue stripe on the side of her car. Mr Fleming and Mr Marx have silver stripes on the sides of their cars. Miss Jenkins' and Mr Fleming's have blue upholstery, the others have white.

20. Who has a car with blue upholstery and a silver stripe?

a) Mr Bagshaw b) Miss Jenkins c) Mrs Chance
d) Mr Fleming e) Mr Marx

21. Who has a car with a silver stripe and white upholstery?

a) Mr Bagshaw b) Miss Jenkins c) Mrs Chance
d) Mr Fleming e) Mr Marx

22. Who has got the red car with a blue stripe and matching upholstery?

a) Mr Bagshaw b) Miss Jenkins c) Mrs Chance
d) Mr Fleming e) Mr Marx

K. In a 'knockout' basketball competition, Centurions are beaten by Raiders. Saracens beat Centurions. Saracens are beaten by Raiders and Aztecs. Centurions and Raiders are beaten by Aztecs.

23. How many games do Saracens win?

a) 1 b) 2 c) 3
d) 4 e) 0

24. How many games do Raiders win?

a) 1 b) 2 c) 3
d) 4 e) 0

25. Who emerges as the champions?

a) Raiders b) Saracens c) Aztecs
d) Centurions

L. Stopping at the shop on the way to school, Cheryl and Tom are the only ones not to buy chocolate. Of the five children, four of them, including Laura, buy fudge. Unlike the others, Sally, Cheryl and Sandy do not buy any toffee. In fact, Cheryl only buys fruit gums as she does not like other kinds of sweets.

26. Who only had a piece of toffee and a piece of fudge?

    a) Sally b) Cheryl c) Laura
    d) Tom e) Sandy

27. Who had three sweets?

    a) Sally b) Cheryl c) Laura
    d) Tom e) Sandy

28. Who are the two people who took the same number and type of sweets?

    a) Sally and Laura b) Sandy and Laura c) Laura and Tom
    d) Tom and Sandy e) Sandy and Sally

29. In total, how many sweets were taken by the group?

    a) 7 b) 8 c) 9
    d) 10 e) 11 f) 12

M. Jane, Rachel and Tessa are girls who are wearing a jacket, coat or skirt in blue, green or red. None of these articles of clothing is the same colour and each girl is wearing a different colour. The coat belonging to Tessa is not green. Rachel's jacket and Jane's skirt are the same colour. Tessa's skirt is red. Her jacket, Rachel's skirt and Jane's coat are all the same colour.

30. What colour is Tessa's coat?

    a) blue b) green c) red

31. What colour is Jane's jacket?

    a) blue b) green c) red

32. Which girl has the green coat?

    a) Jane b) Rachel c) Tessa

33. Which girl has the blue jacket?

    a) Jane b) Rachel c) Tessa

Answers

1. c	7. d	13. a	19. a	25. c	31. c
2. a	8. b	14. e	20. d	26. d	32. a
3. d	9. b	15. c	21. e	27. c	33. b
4. d	10. d	16. b	22. b	28. e	
5. b	11. d	17. b	23. a	29. d	
6. f	12. a	18. c	24. b	30. a	

Scoring

Number right minus number wrong = __________

Plus 4 aged under 16, plus 2 if aged 17–20 + __________

Score on the test = __________

Use the following table to convert your test score to a score out of 10 or 'sten score'. You can then enter your 'sten score' in the chart on page 200.

Test score	1–4	5–6	7–8	9–10	11–13	14–19	20–23	24–27	28–29	30+
Sten score	1	2	3	4	5	6	7	8	9	10

Part 4

Physical tests

The tests in this section are representative of a type that have been used with great success by occupational psychologists. Over many years organizations have sought people with a natural aptitude for understanding the cause and effect of physical forces, so that these can be acted upon in concrete ways. These tests give evidence of the potential to apply intelligence to make things happen. Although talent in both areas may be realized in all sorts of practical ways, the long-term career path will also depend upon the strength of your other visual and numerical skills, which can complement and extend your potential further.

Test 8, Dynamics, presents mechanical problems as well as others connected with forces. It may at first glance seem strange, but relatively little in the way of past experience is required if you have the underlying aptitude to solve these problems. This is why the test has been particularly useful in identifying people for engineering and related disciplines, especially among women whose education may have disadvantaged them in relation to men, who were, historically, more likely to have been exposed to mechanics.

Test 9, Information Processing, requires an aptitude to trace through a pattern without deviating from the core of the problem. An important element is the ability to maintain focus and control. If you do better on this test than test 8 you are more likely to be drawn to the more schematic areas of engineering and planning connected with electrics, electronics, diagrams and computer hardware.

Test 8

Dynamics

This tests your understanding of how things work. There is a written question and a drawing. Together, they contain all the information you need to answer the question.

Example

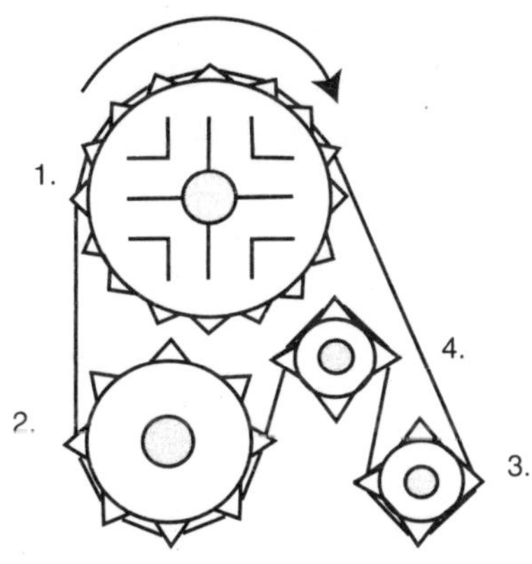

A chain is passed around four wheels, 1, 2, 3 and 4, so that the large wheel, 2, moves clockwise. Which of the wheels turns anti-clockwise?

a) 1 b) 2 c) 3 d) 4 e) none

The answer is 4.

You can do the items in any order you like. Do not mark this book if it is not your own, but record your answers and any working out you need to do on separate paper. If you wish to gain an estimate of your aptitude, record the number of the question you are on after exactly 10 minutes. Otherwise, take as long as you wish to complete the items.

Timed test: 10 minutes

1. Which ball is heaviest?

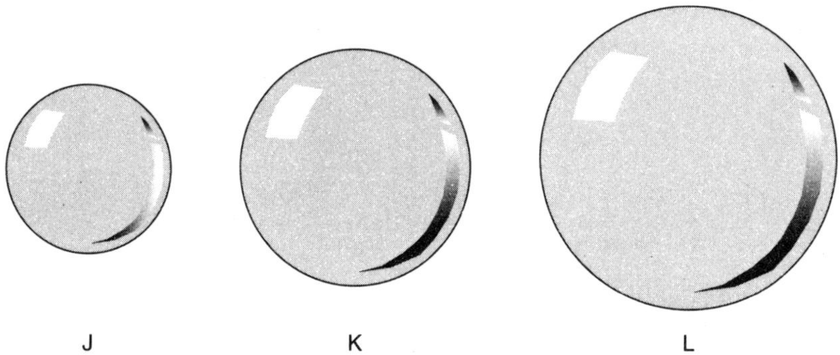

a) All weigh the same b) L is heaviest c) cannot say d) J is heaviest

2. Three rubber wheels, A, B and C are touching so that if one moves the others must also move. If wheel A turns clockwise, which way will wheel C turn?

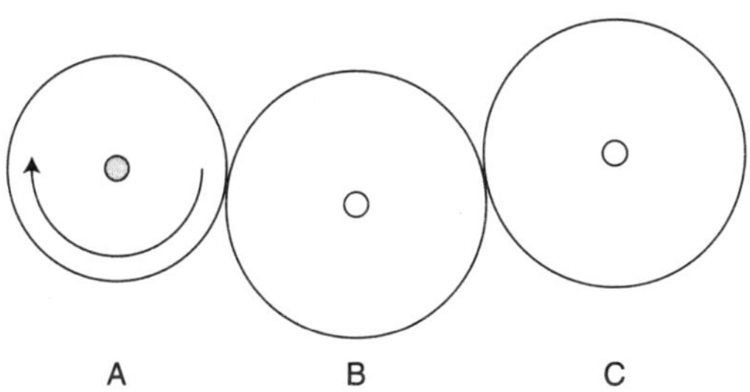

a) anti-clockwise b) all the same way c) clockwise d) none will turn

3. A section through a dam is shown. At which point is the dam strongest?

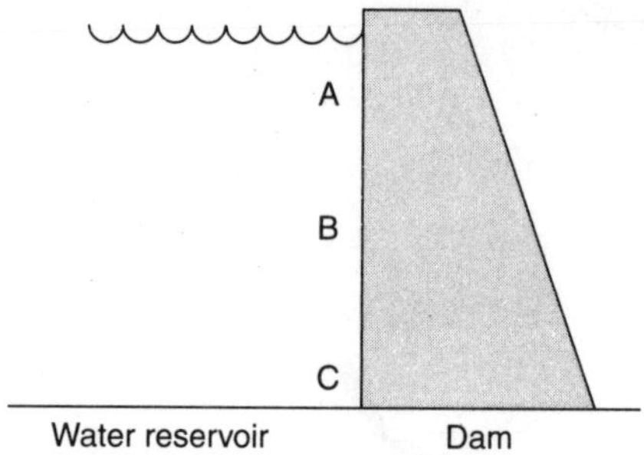

a) At point A b) At point B c) At point C d) All equally

4. In the same dam, at which point is the water coldest?

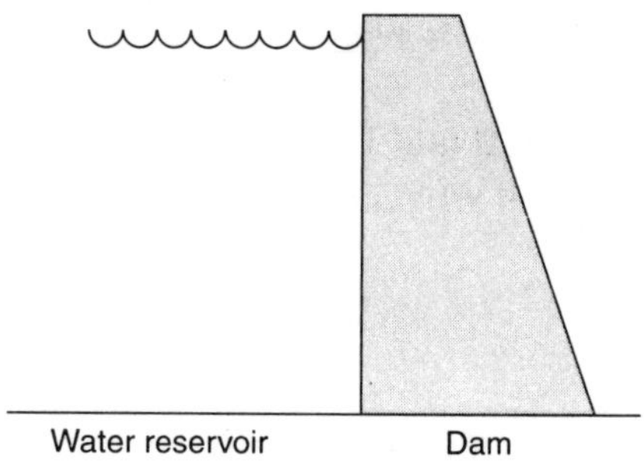

a) At point A b) At point B c) At point C d) All equally

5. The beam is twice as thick at one end as the other. At what point can it be placed on the wall, and at a right angle to the wall, so that it balances?

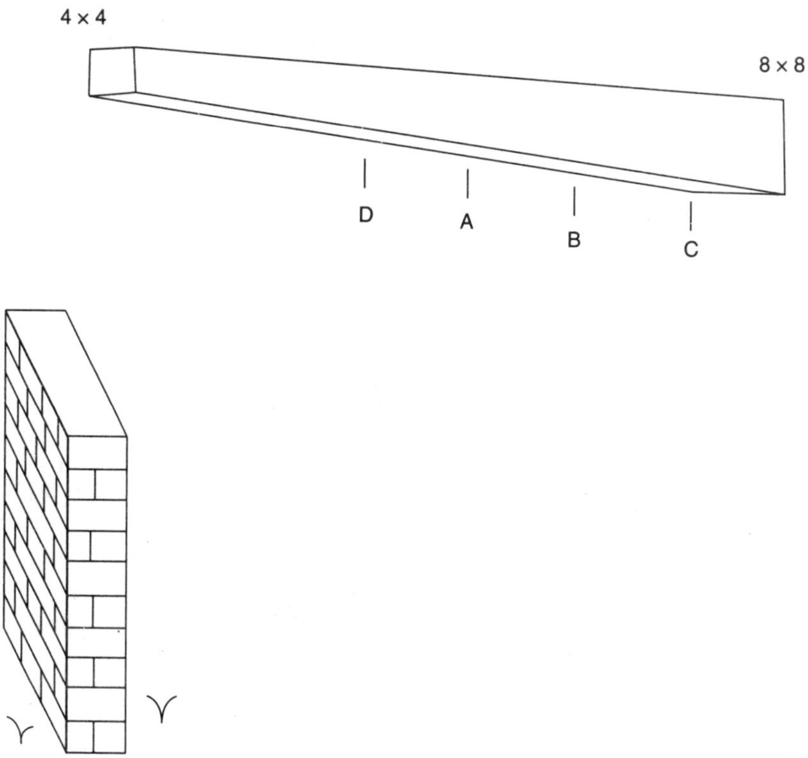

a) point A b) point B c) point C d) needs support at both ends

6. When rays of light hit a lens, in which direction do they continue?

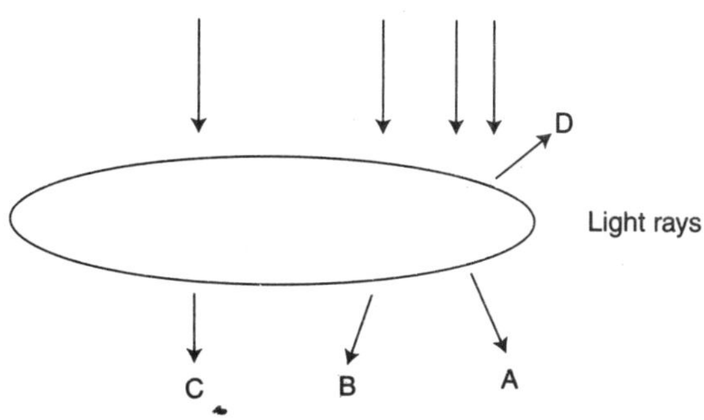

a) A b) B c) C d) D

7. A band passes around all the wheels so that they can all be turned by the driving wheel. When the driving wheel turns clockwise, which way does wheel W turn?

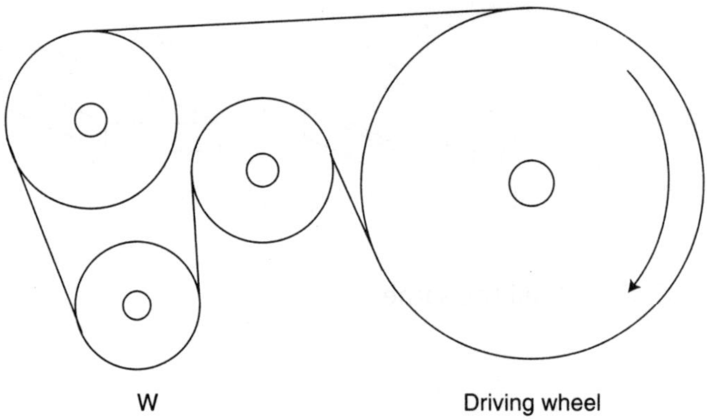

a) clockwise b) cannot move c) anti-clockwise d) either way

8. The drawing shows a cross-section of a wall, with a shelf upright against it. By means of a hinge, the shelf can be folded upright against the wall. It can be let down to the horizontal, being held at point H by a rope, which is suspended from a hook, A, B or C. When the shelf is let down and supported by the rope, which hook is least likely to be pulled out of the wall?

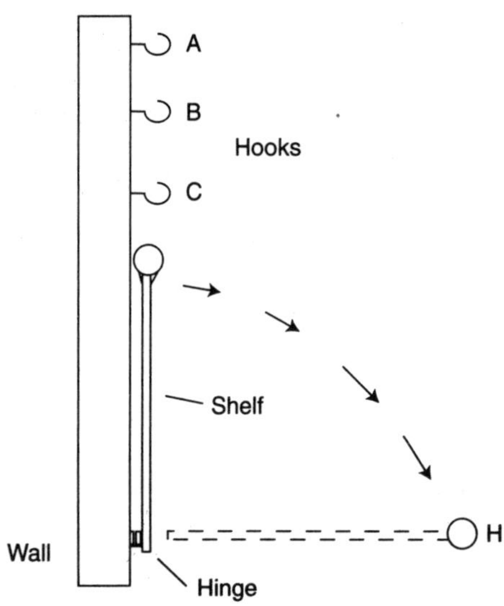

9. If the three iron bars are all the same length, which one will support the greatest weight?

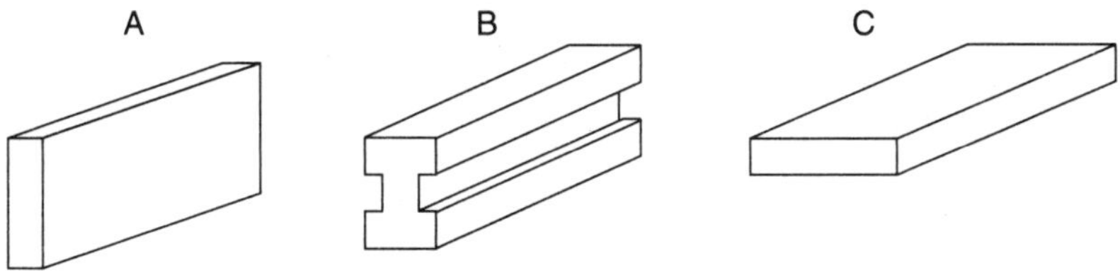

a) A b) B c) C d) all the same

10. Three racing cars travel at equal speed round the built-up curve of a bend. Which car is most likely to slip?

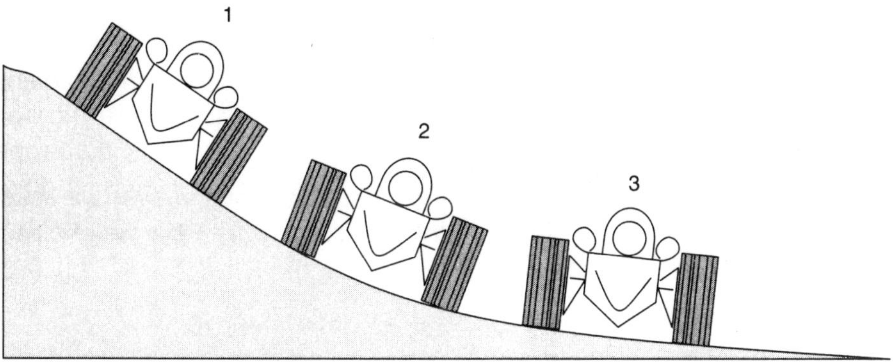

☐ ☐ ☐ ☐

a) 1 b) 2 c) 3 d) all the same

11. If three racing cars are level with each other, side by side as they go into the bend, and all are also level as they come out of the bend, which car is travelling fastest?

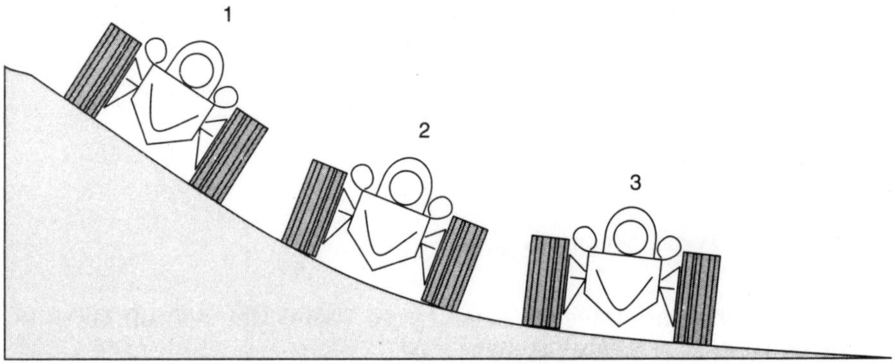

☐ ☐ ☐ ☐

a) 1 b) 2 c) 3 d) all the same

12. This old fashioned 'grandfather clock' pendulum and weight are made of iron. To keep correct time, in which direction might the weight need to be adjusted in Summer?

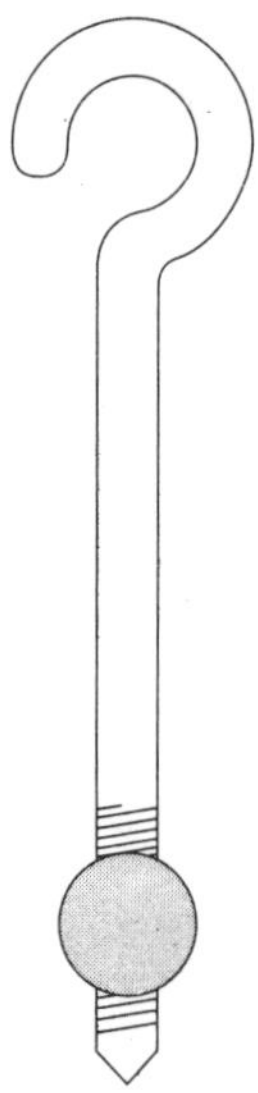

a) upwards b) will not need adjustment c) downwards

13. To lever up the large, heavy weight with the least effort, by pushing down in the direction of the arrow, at which point under the beam should the block be placed?

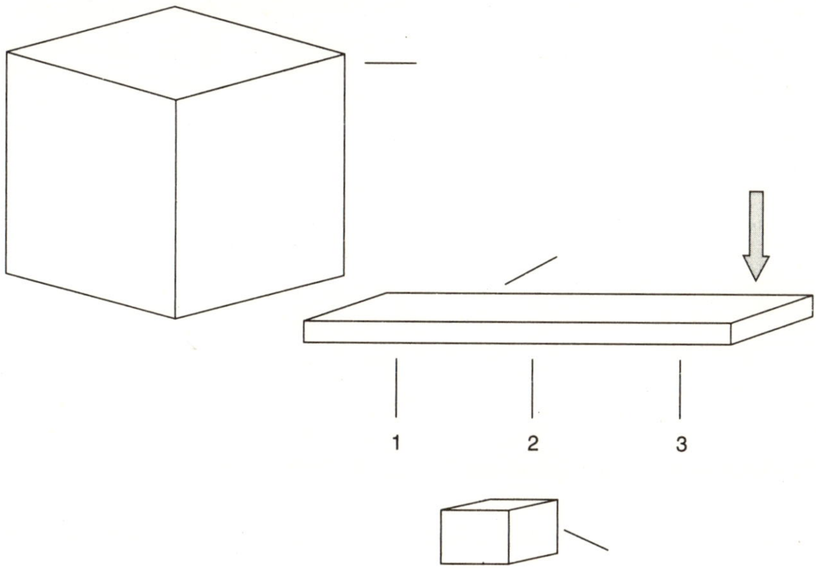

a) 1 b) 2 c) 3 d) makes no difference

14. A heavy metal bar is fixed inside a cardboard tube. When the tube is placed on a slope, as shown, which direction will the tube roll?

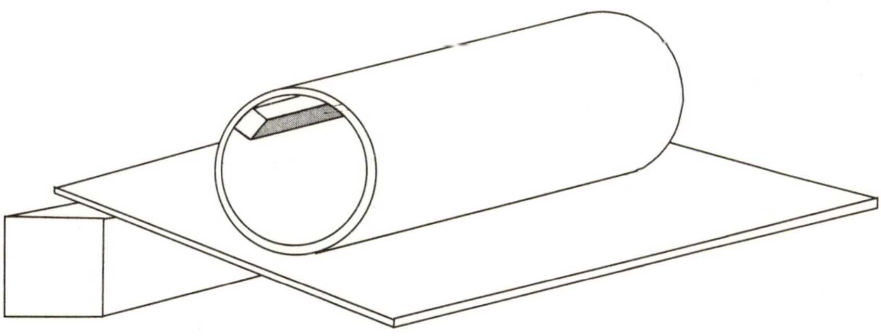

a) down the slope b) up the slope c) stay still

15. When the driving wheel 1 turns in the direction shown, wheel 2 turns…

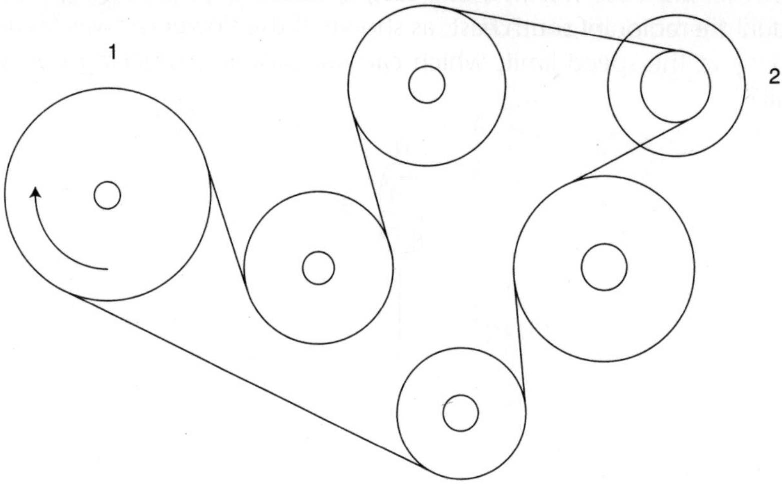

a) anti-clockwise? b) clockwise? c) system jams?

16. Assuming that the belt and wheels did not jam, which wheel would turn fastest?

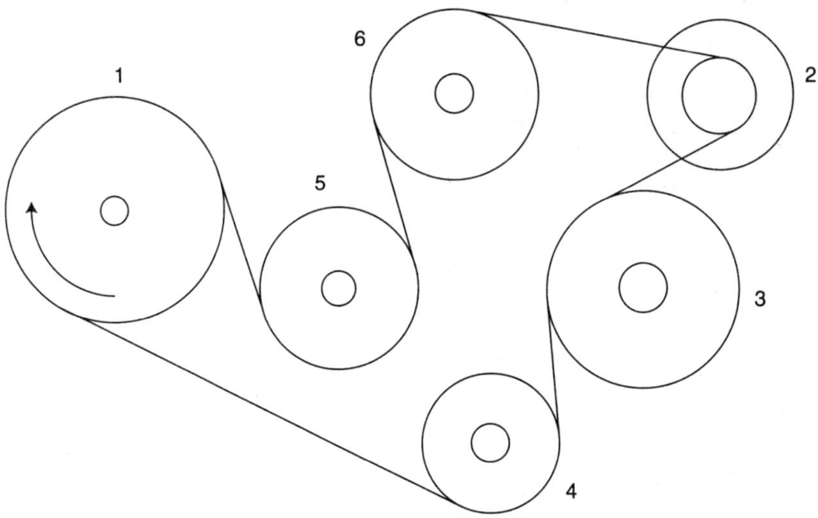

a) 1 b) 2 c) 3 d) 4 e) 5 f) 6

17. Two cars, A and B, one travelling from the North, N, due south, S, and the other from the west, W, due east, E, collide at point P. They come to rest in the region of south east, as shown. If the slower car was travelling exactly at the speed limit, which car was probably breaking the speed limit?

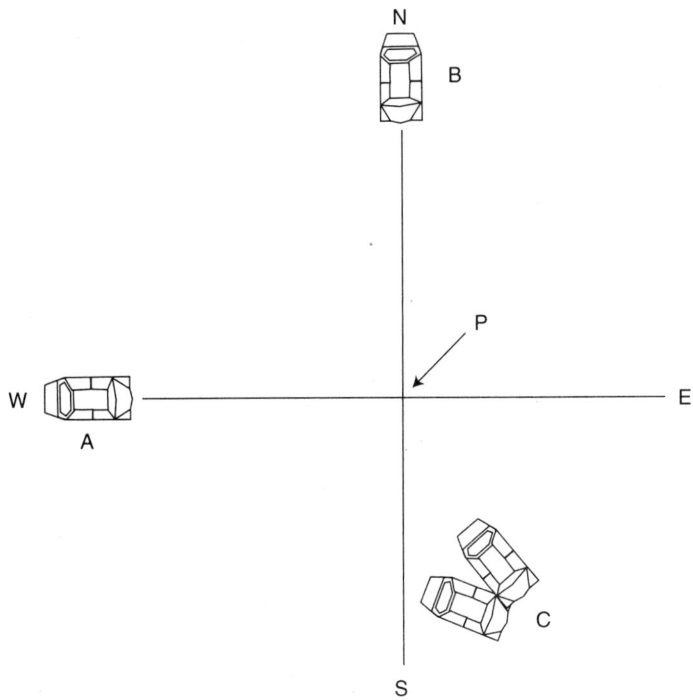

a) A b) B c) cannot tell

18. The ladders, 1 and 2, and the walls are viewed from the side. Which ladder is safer when climbed?

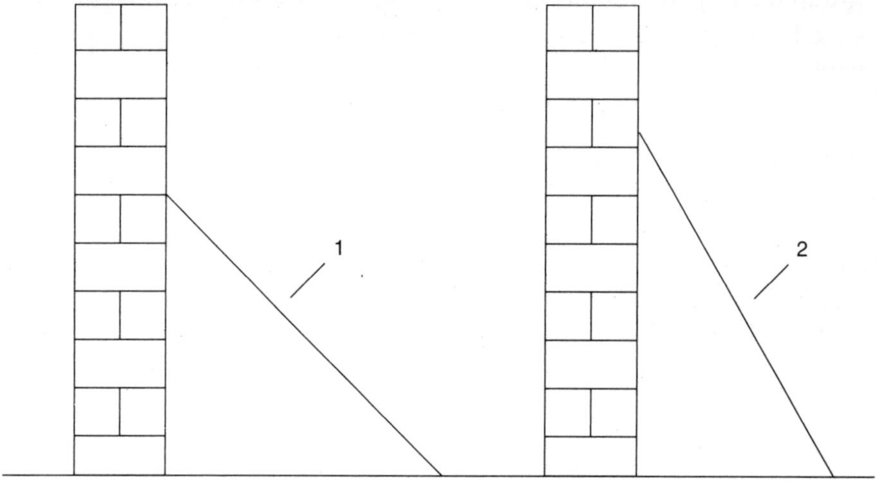

a) 1 b) 2 c) both the same

19. In a hot-water cylinder, from which outlet should hot water be taken?

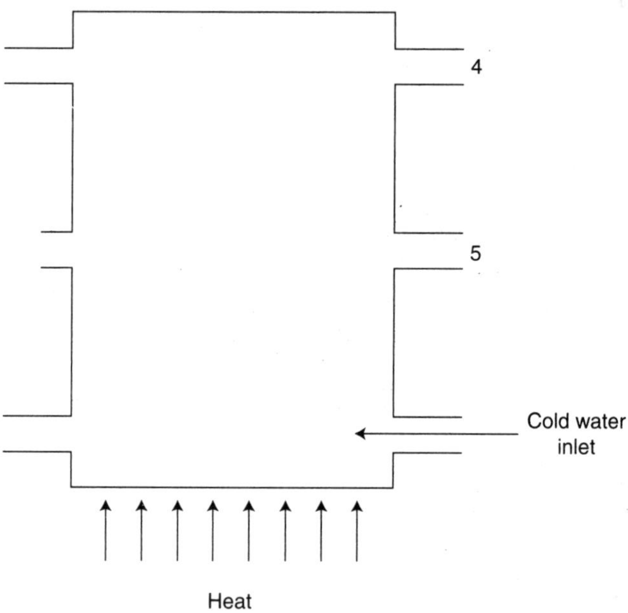

a) 1 b) 2 c) 3 d) 4 e) 5 f) does not matter

20. When the spacecraft is not affected by the Earth's gravity, and the thrust of the rocket is zero, the astronaut will:

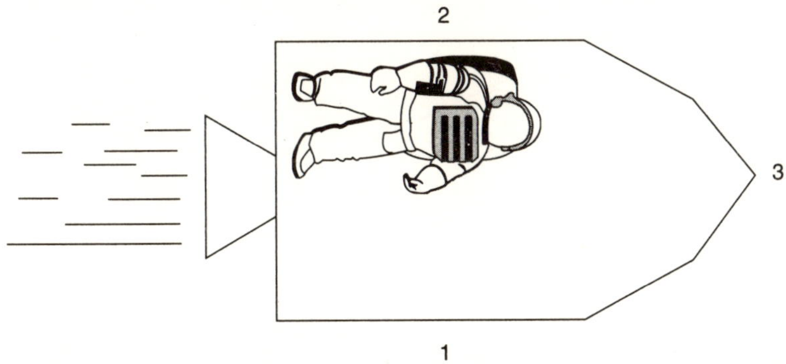

a) fall to side 1 b) stay where he is at side 2
c) be thrust towards the nose at 3

21. In space, when the stationary vehicle accelerates, the spaceman will:

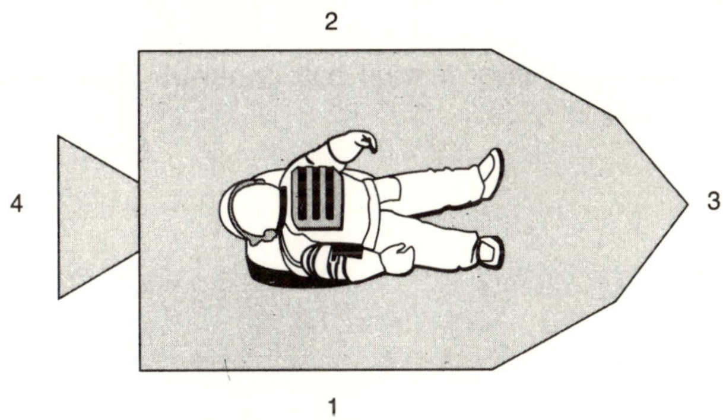

a) be thrust towards the nose at 3 b) fall down towards side 1
c) float upwards, due to weightlessness, towards 2
d) fall on his head on the floor at side 4

22. When wheel 1 turns clockwise, which way does wheel 4 turn?

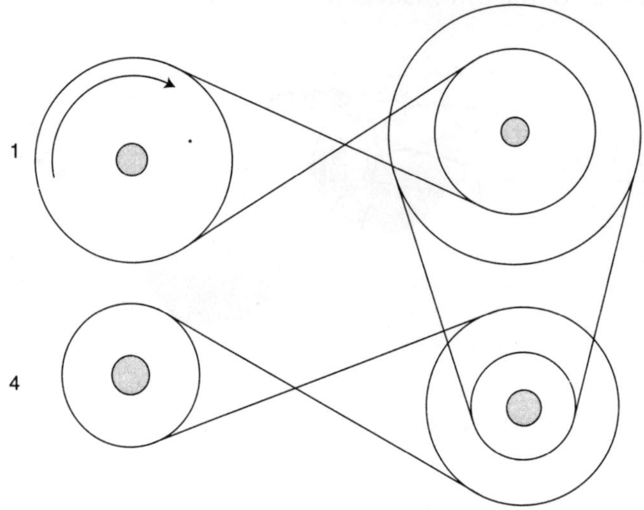

a) clockwise b) anti-clockwise c) system jams

23. In which direction does a steel ball continue after impact on a rigid, heavy steel block?

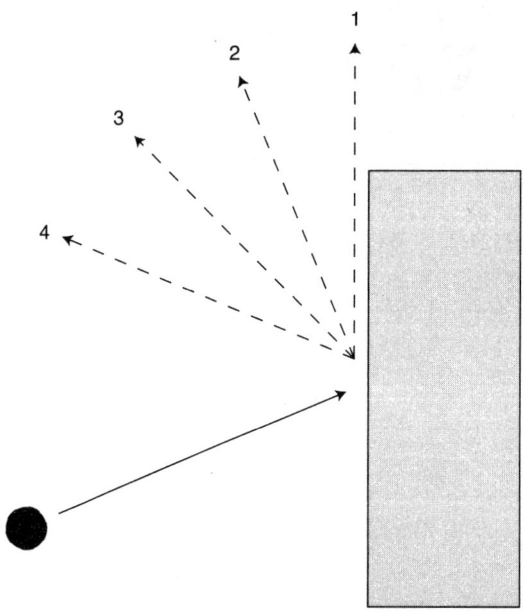

a) 1 b) 2 c) 3 d) 4

24. In which direction will ball 3 move when ball 1 is struck as shown?

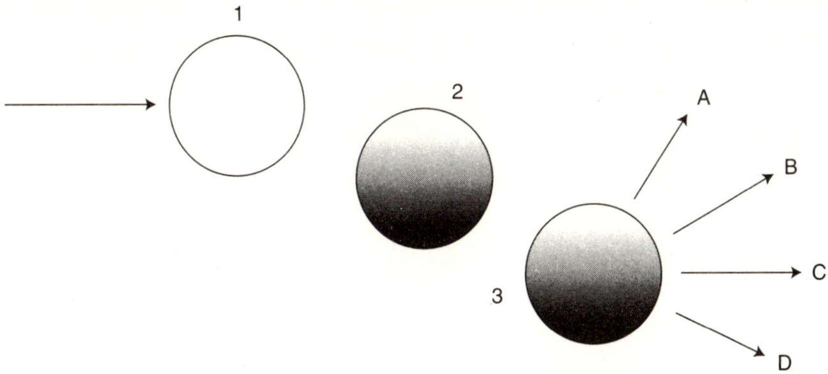

a) A b) B c) C d) D e) 3 stays where it is

25. Which way will helical gear H turn when helical gear M turns as shown?

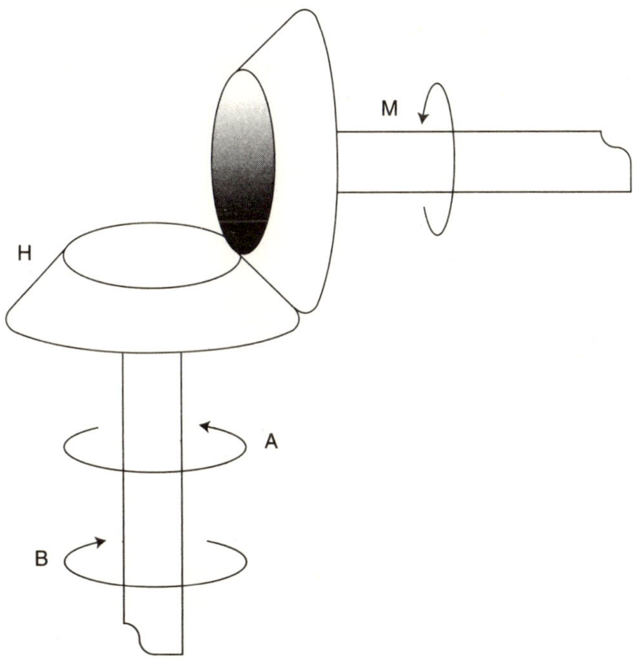

a) A b) B c) either way

Answers

1. c	6. a	11. a	16. b	21. d
2. c	7. a	12. a	17. b	22. a
3. c	8. a	13. a	18. b	23. d
4. c	9. b	14. b	19. c	24. c
5. b	10. c	15. b	20. b	25. b

Scoring

Number right minus number wrong = __________

Plus 2 aged under 16, plus 1 if aged 17–20 + __________

Score on the test = __________

Use the following table to convert your test score to a score out of 10 or 'sten score'. You can then enter your 'sten score' in the chart on page 200.

Test score	1–5	6–7	8–9	10–11	12–13	14–15	16–17	18–19	20–21	22+
Sten score	1	2	3	4	5	6	7	8	9	10

Test 9

Tracing

In this test, you have to follow a line from the left-hand side of the page until you arrive at the right-hand side. Each line goes straight across other lines it comes to. Sometimes the line returns across the page before ending on the right-hand side. Where the line ends is a small picture or symbol.

Your task is to locate the symbol in the chart and see what letter is underneath it. Then, you tick the box underneath that letter where the line first started on the left hand side of the page. In the example below, you can see the chart with pictures and letters. A letter goes with each picture.

On the left-hand side of the page are boxes underneath letters where you have to place your tick. If you start with the first box and follow the line along, you will see that it comes out at a picture of a heart. In the chart, underneath the heart, is the letter 'd'. So, 'd' has been ticked in the box where the line started. Try the other lines yourself.

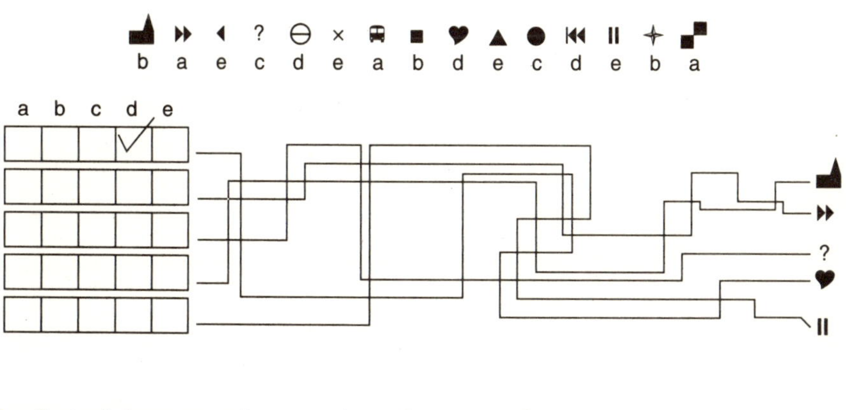

The first of the examples was done for you – the answer was 'd'. The answer to the next is 'a', then 'c', then 'b' and 'e'.

The test on the next page is done in just the same way. Work as quickly as you can. If this is not your book record your answers on a separate sheet of paper.

Timed test: 5 minutes

9	A	Σ	H	ϑ	#	Z	5	σ	λ	ν	μ	4	8	0
b	a	e	c	d	e	a	b	d	e	c	d	e	b	a

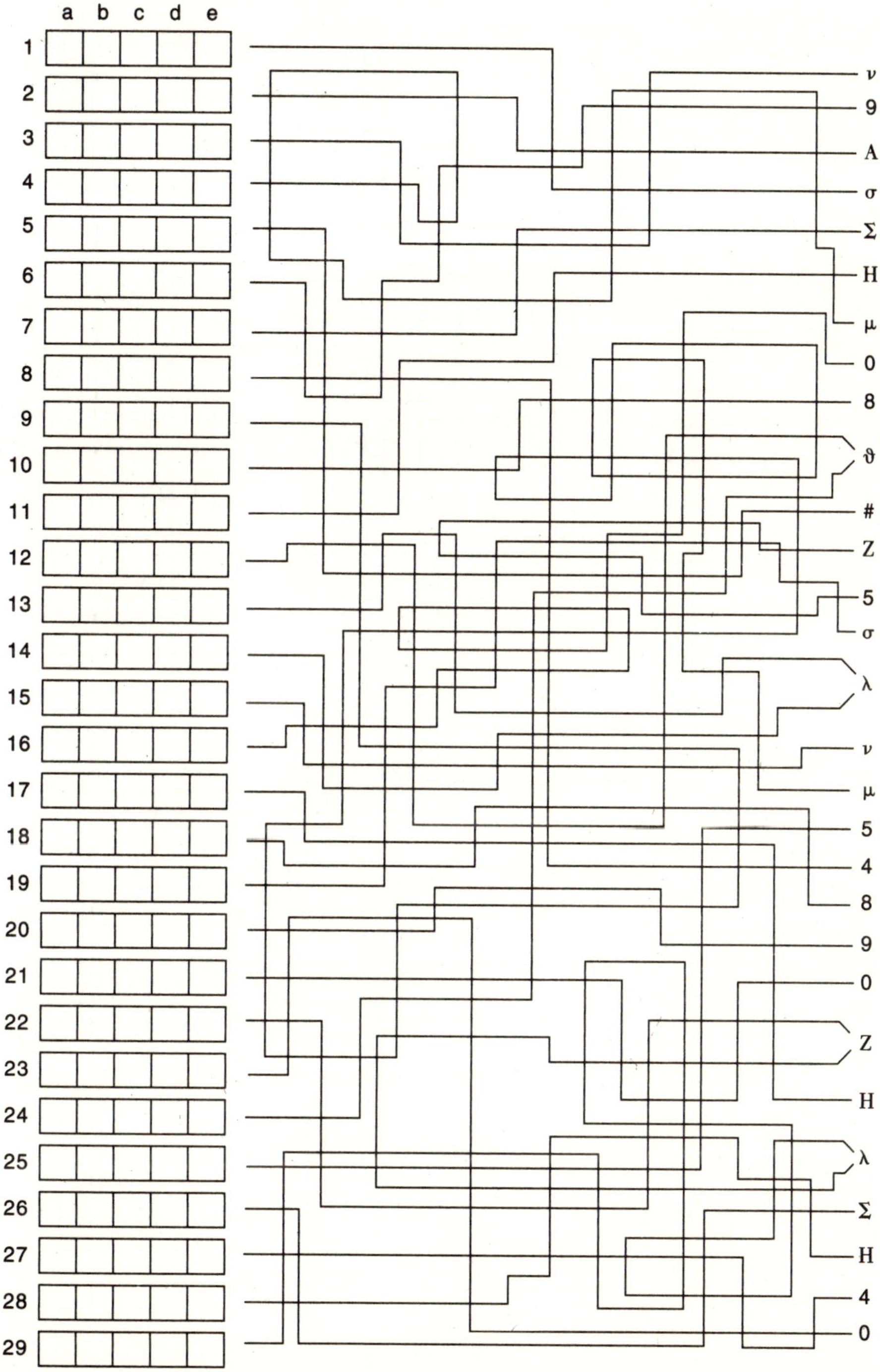

9	A	Σ	H	ϑ	#	Z	5	σ	λ	ν	μ	4	8	0
b	a	e	c	d	e	a	b	d	e	c	d	e	b	a

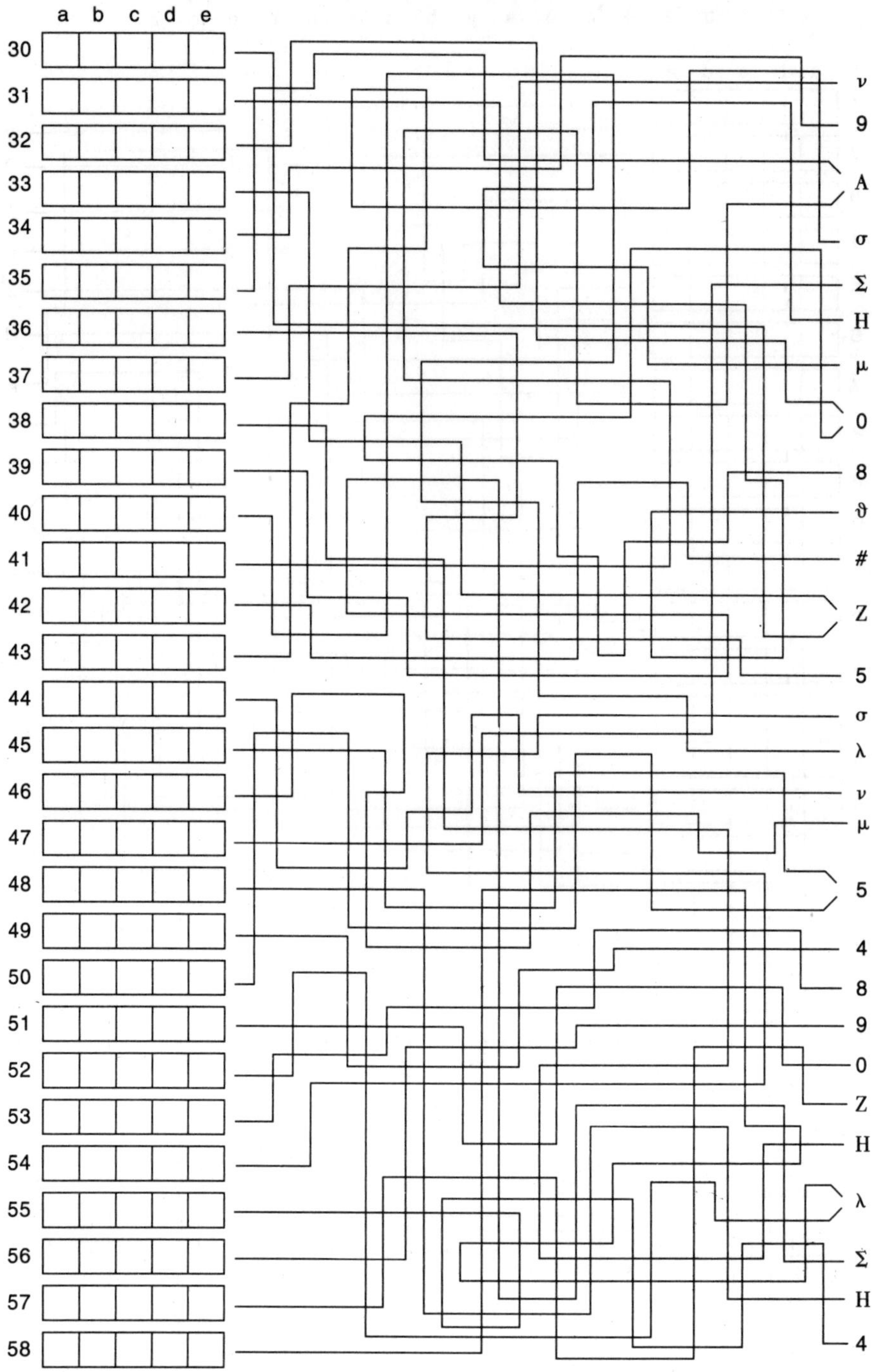

Answers

1. d	11. c	21. a	31. d	41. a	51. a
2. a	12. c	22. a	32. a	42. e	52. e
3. c	13. d	23. a	33. a	43. d	53. b
4. d	14. e	24. d	34. b	44. c	54. d
5. e	15. c	25. b	35. a	45. b	55. e
6. b	16. a	26. e	36. b	46. d	56. b
7. e	17. c	27. e	37. c	47. e	57. a
8. e	18. b	28. c	38. c	48. c	58. e
9. d	19. d	29. e	39. e	49. e	
10. b	20. b	30. a	40. e	50. b	

Scoring

Number right minus number wrong = __________

Plus 2 if aged under 16 + __________

Score on the test = __________

Use the following table to convert your test score to a score out of 10 or 'sten score'. You can then enter your 'sten score' in the chart on page 200.

Test score	1–20	21–23	24–26	27–29	30–32	33–35	36–38	39–41	42–44	45+
Sten score	1	2	3	4	5	6	7	8	9	10

Part 5

Spatial tests

The tests in this section require you to 'see' an object in your mind. Not only that, but to 'move' the object in your mind, so that you can see what it looks like from behind and also when it is upside down. Being able to recognize shapes and their dimensions is a talent that can have all manner of imaginative visual applications. In psychological terms it can often point to flexibility of thought and, of course, artistic creativity. The ability to accurately discriminate among rotating and changing shapes in some way replicates how many people 'turn things over in their mind'. Original possibilities and outcomes often arise from this process. If you do well on this test you may well be the type of person who thinks laterally or 'out of the box'.

Test 10, Formation, asks you to choose between different abstract shapes, the purpose being to assess your talent for judging the orientation of lines, contours and forms. Potential here may be expressed in some artistic form, literally in art and design, but, depending upon other talents that may emerge on the other tests, could be applied to areas of technology or geography, if you are numerically minded as well, or to writing or media work, if your strength is also on the verbal side.

Test 11, 3D, makes similar demands as the test of Formation, but the shapes themselves are regular and retain their dimensions. They do not demand the same 'flow' as the test of Formation, but do ask for a structured approach to the solution of the problem that has more in common with tasks associated with planning, architecture and with all sorts of design work. Again, unlike the Formation test, the specifically three-dimensional problems ask you to 'look behind what appears on the surface of things'. You have to conceptualize a diagram that exists nowhere else but in your own mind. Generally, people who do well on this test are almost always recognized as intelligent, even if they are unexceptional in their conventional education, so they often do well when they have left school.

Test 10

Formation

This test explores how easily you can 'see' and turn around objects in your mind.

You are shown a shape in the middle of the page. Below it are five other shapes. Each of these is numbered. You have to decide whether each of the alternatives is identical to the original shape. It will still be identical to the original if it has been turned over or around. It will not be the same as the original if the proportions or parts have been changed. You are to answer each question with a 'Y' for 'Yes' and 'N' for 'No'. If each shape is not exactly the same or a 'mirror image' you mark 'N' for 'No'. Try to 'see' the shape in your mind.

Example

1 2 3 4 5

Answers to example items: 1 N; 2 N; 3 Y; 4 Y; 5 Y

Do not mark this book if it is not your own, but record your answers and any working out you need to do on separate paper. If you wish to gain an estimate of your aptitude, record the number of the question you are on after exactly 10 minutes. Otherwise, take as long as you wish to complete the items.

Timed test: 10 minutes

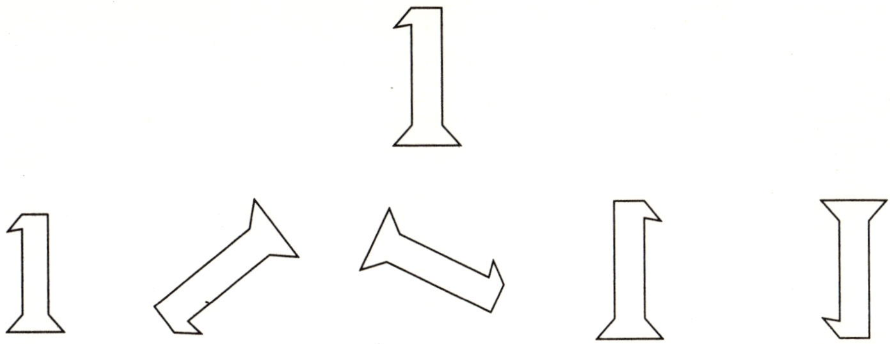

1 2 3 4 5

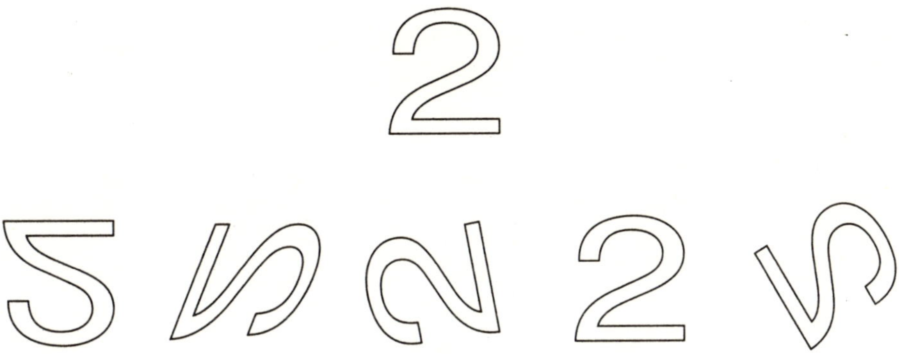

6 7 8 9 10

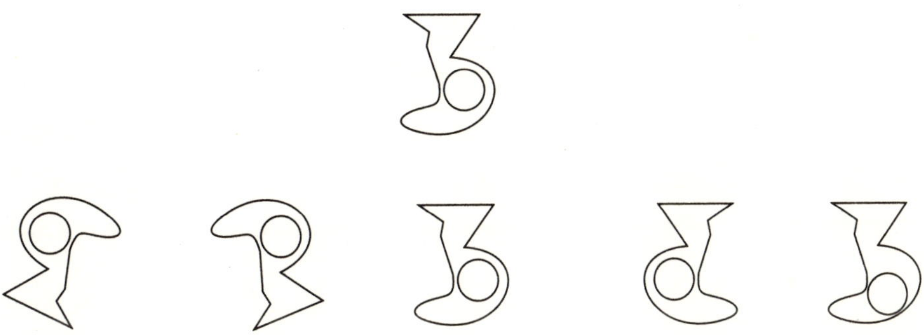

11 12 13 14 15

16 17 18 19 20

21 22 23 24 25

26 27 28 29 30

31

32

33

34

35

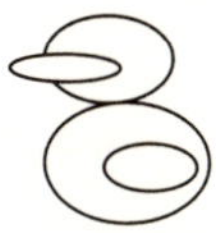

36

37

38

39

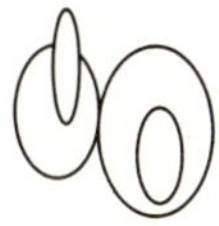

40

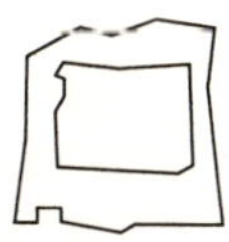

41

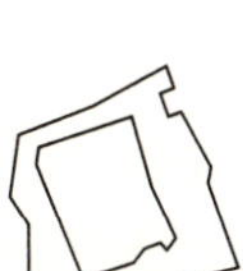

42

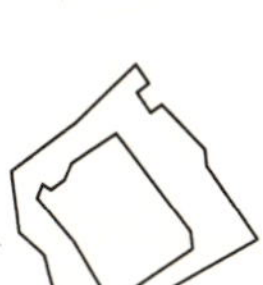

43

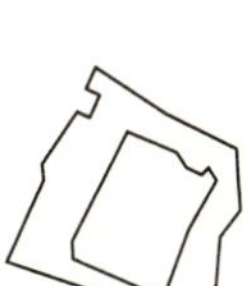

44

45

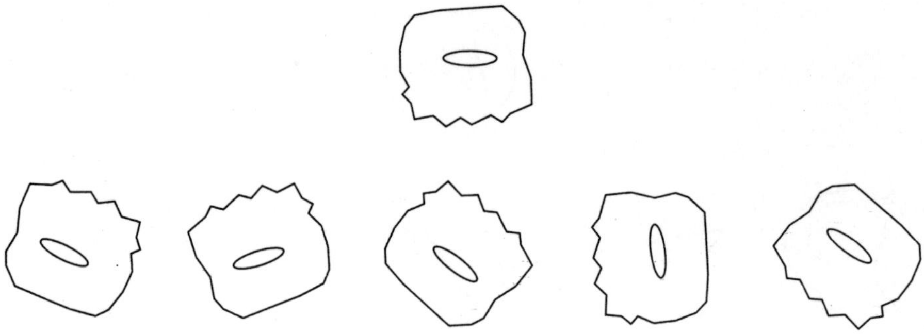

46 47 48 49 50

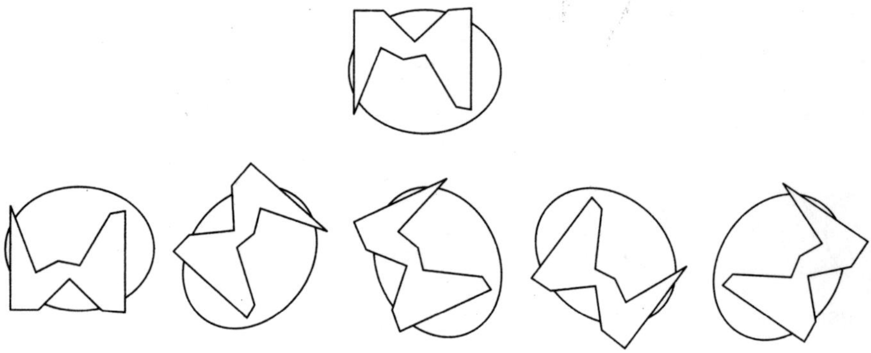

51 52 53 54 55

56 57 58 59 60

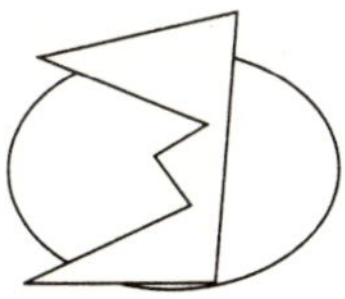

61

62

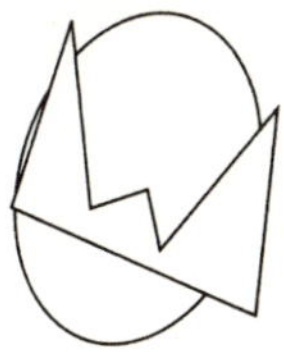

63

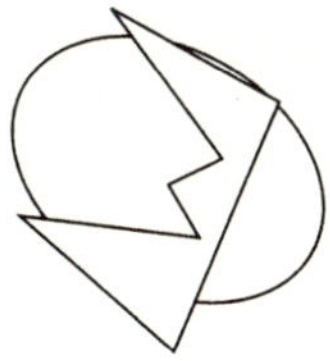

64

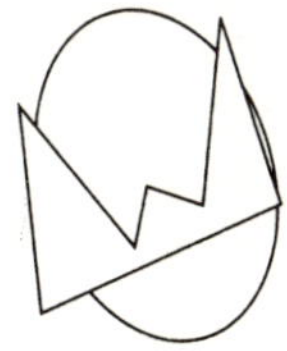

65

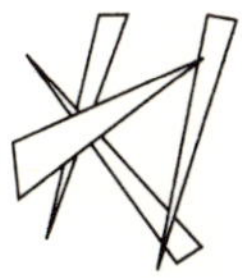

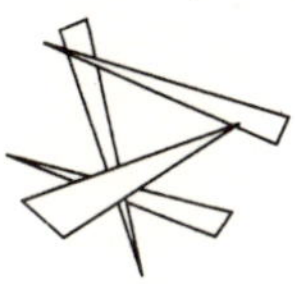

66

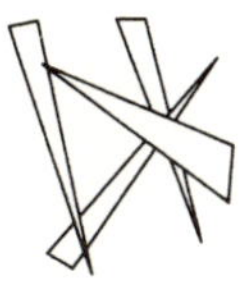

67

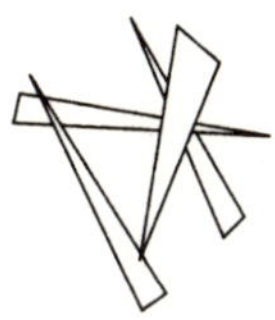

68

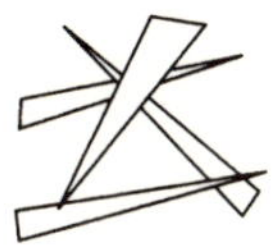

69

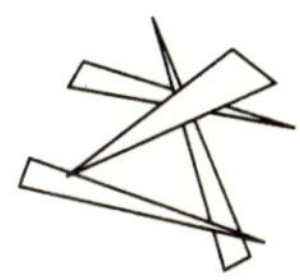

70

Answers

1. N	15. N	29. N	43. Y	57. Y
2. N	16. N	30. Y	44. Y	58. Y
3. Y	17. Y	31. Y	45. N	59. N
4. Y	18. Y	32. N	46. N	60. N
5. Y	19. Y	33. Y	47. Y	61. N
6. Y	20. Y	34. N	48. N	62. N
7. N	21. Y	35. N	49. Y	63. Y
8. N	22. Y	36. Y	50. N	64. Y
9. Y	23. N	37. N	51. N	65. Y
10. Y	24. N	38. N	52. N	66. Y
11. Y	25. Y	39. Y	53. N	67. Y
12. N	26. N	40. Y	54. N	68. Y
13. Y	27. Y	41. N	55. Y	69. Y
14. Y	28. Y	42. N	56. Y	70. Y

Scoring

Number right minus number wrong = __________

Plus 2 aged under 16, plus 1 if aged 17–20 + __________

Score on the test = __________

Use the following table to convert your test score to a score out of 10 or 'sten score'. You can then enter your 'sten score' in the chart on page 200.

Test score	1–6	7–12	13–17	18–21	22–25	26–30	31–35	36–41	42–47	53+
Sten score	1	2	3	4	5	6	7	8	9	10

Test 11

3D tests

In this test you are asked to discover the hidden sides of objects. You are shown a stack of blocks. Each block is exactly the same size. You can see the front, or facing, sides. You can also see the top side. But you cannot see the two sides that are hidden from your view. Nor can you see the bottom, or underneath side. However, you can imagine what the hidden sides and underneath must look like.

In each of the tests, there is a stack of blocks. You have to imagine, out of the five possibilities you are given, which one is the view from Side A. Only one of the five is correct. Then, do the same for Sides B and C. In each set of possibilities, only one is correct, even though it may have been turned around. Tick the correct one.

Timed test: 5 minutes

1.

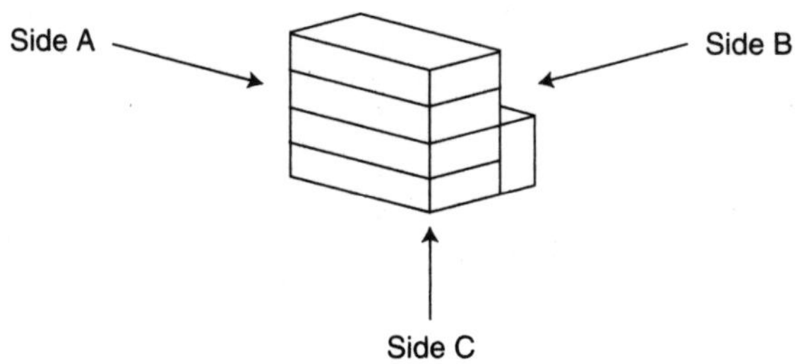

Side A

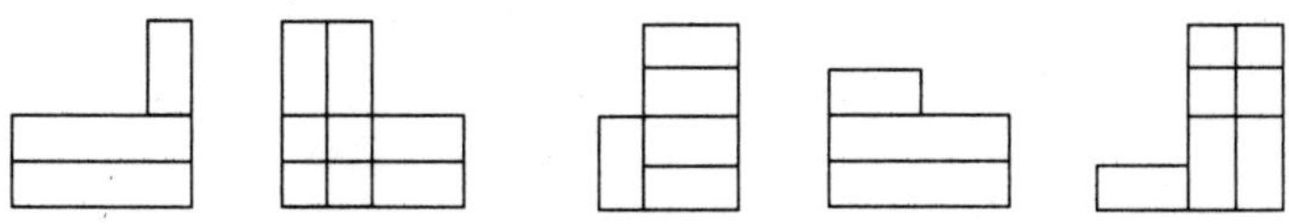

i ii iii iv v

Side B

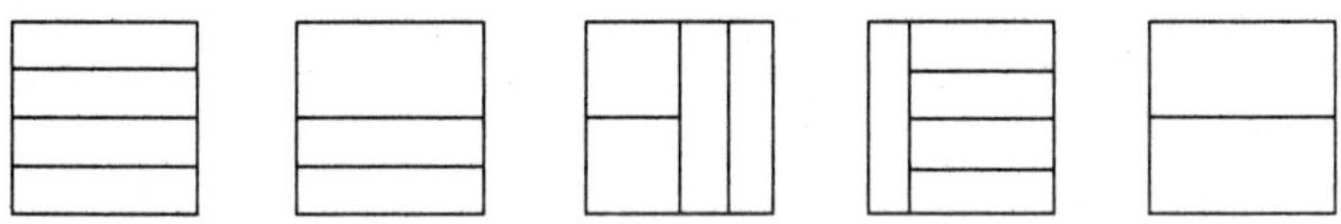

i ii iii iv v

Side C

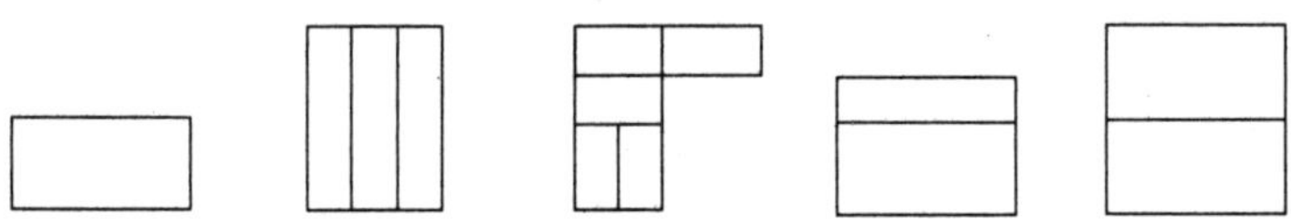

i ii iii iv v

2.

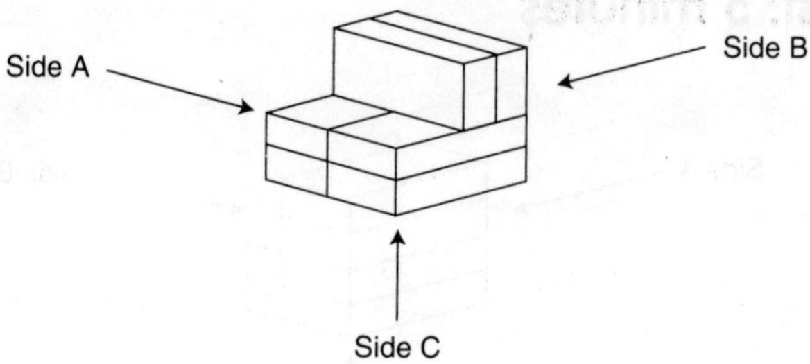

Side A

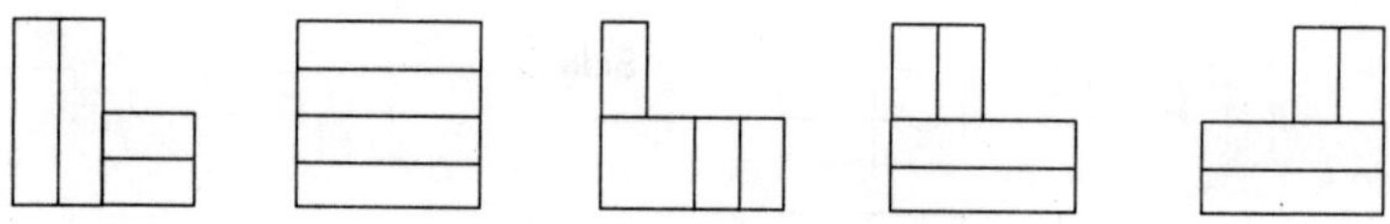

i ii iii iv v

Side B

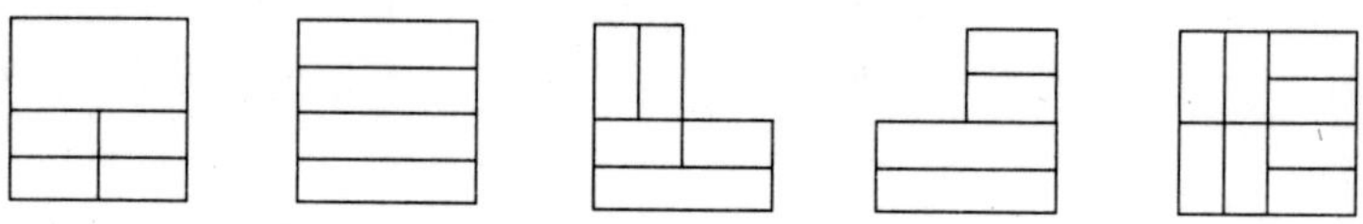

i ii iii iv v

Side C

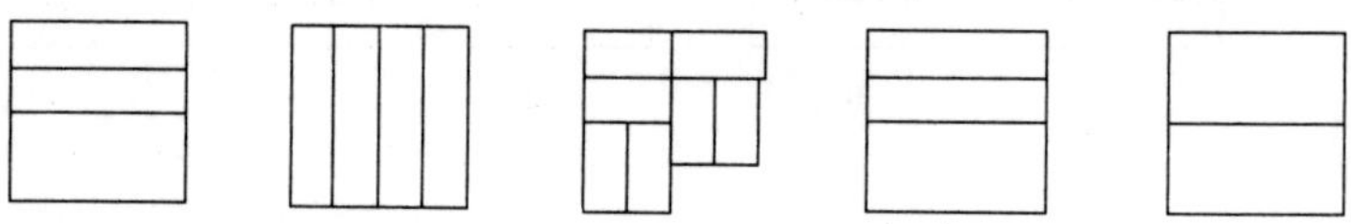

i ii iii iv v

3.

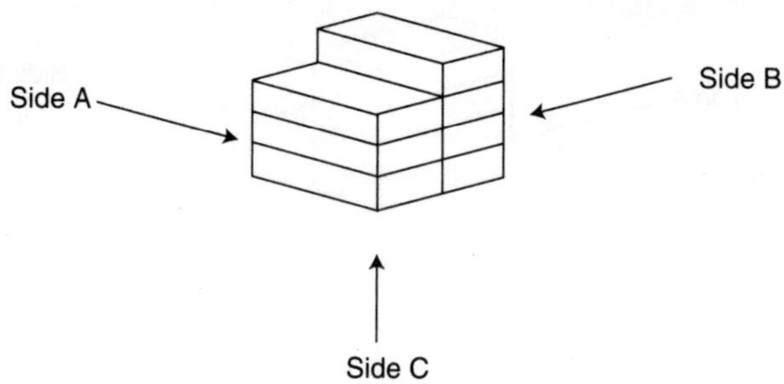

Side A

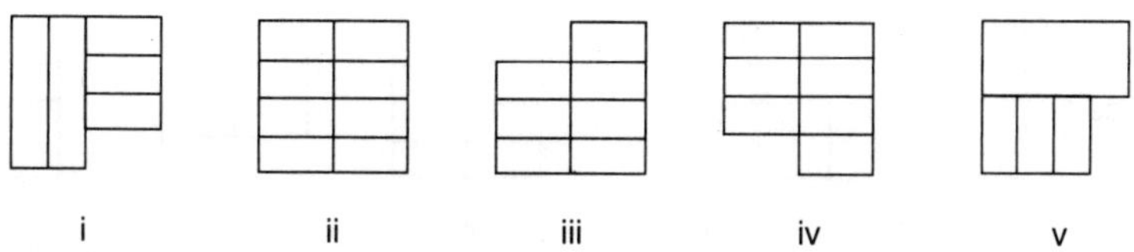

Side B

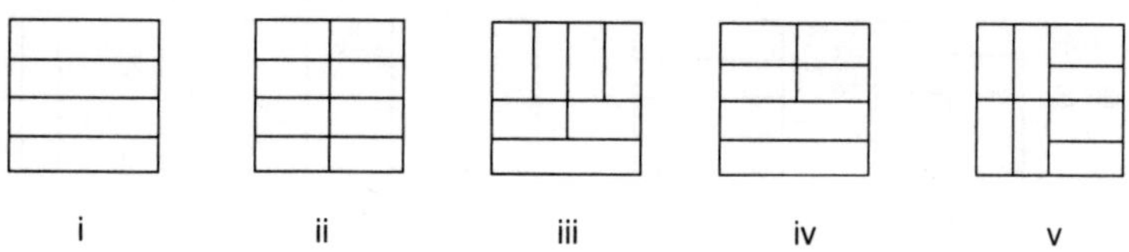

Side C

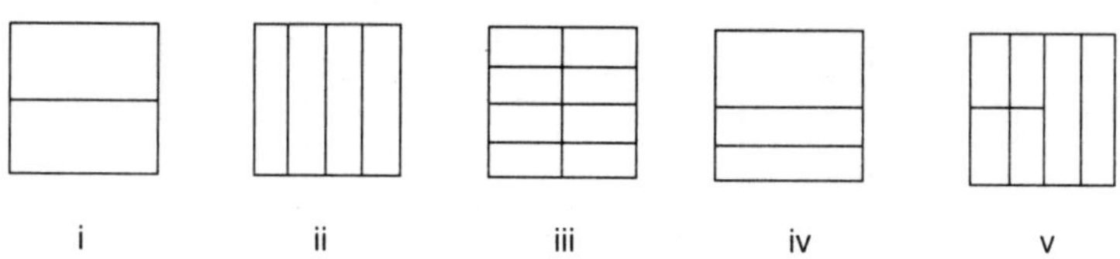

4.

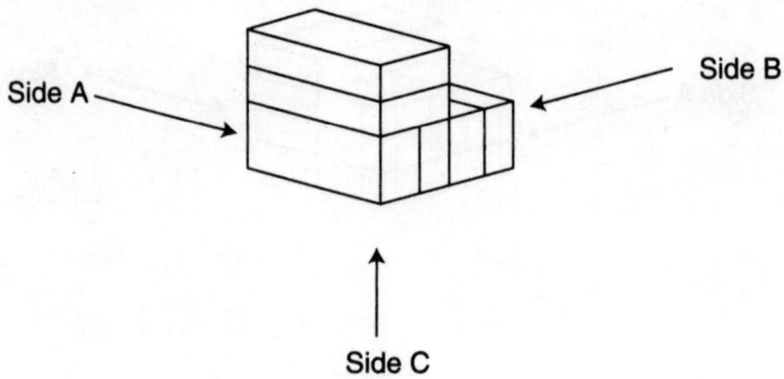

Side A

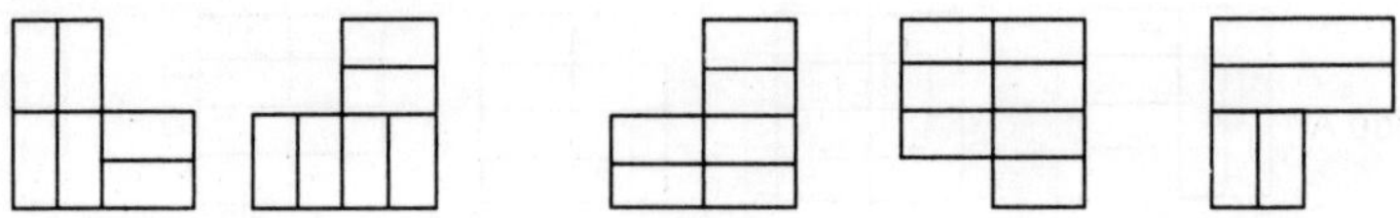

i ii iii iv v

Side B

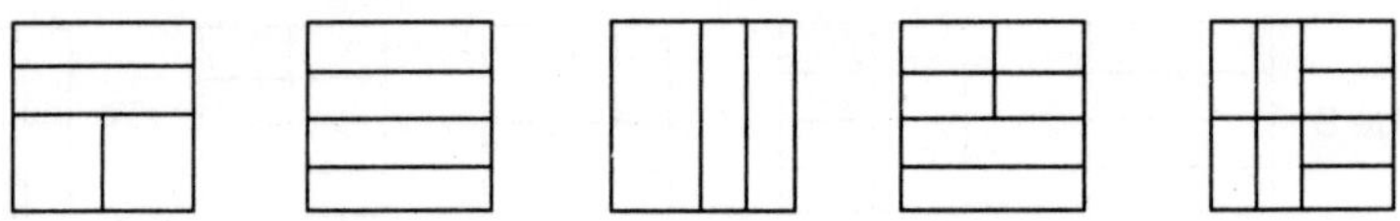

i ii iii iv v

Side C

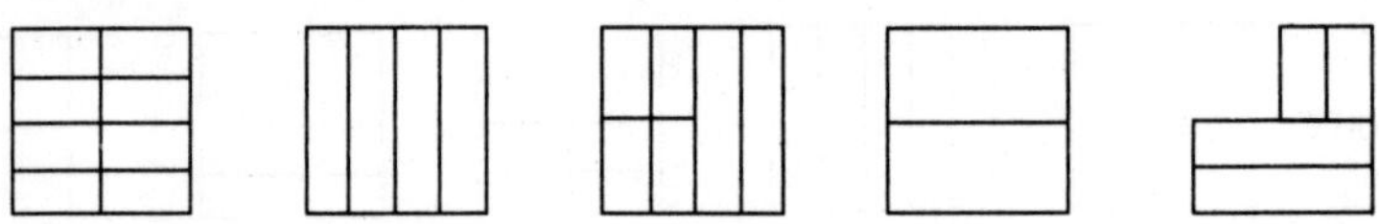

i ii iii iv v

5.

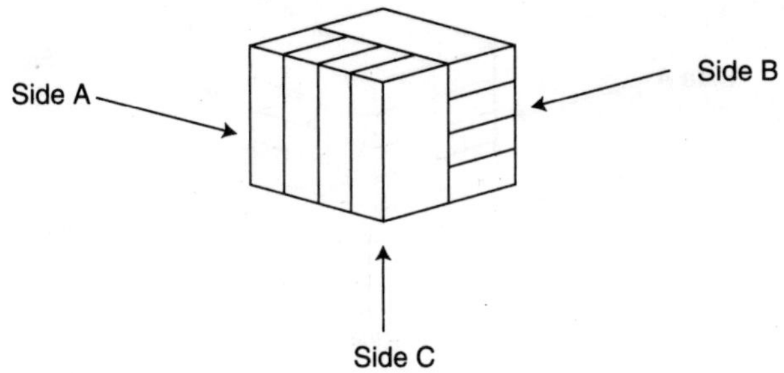
Side A
Side B
Side C

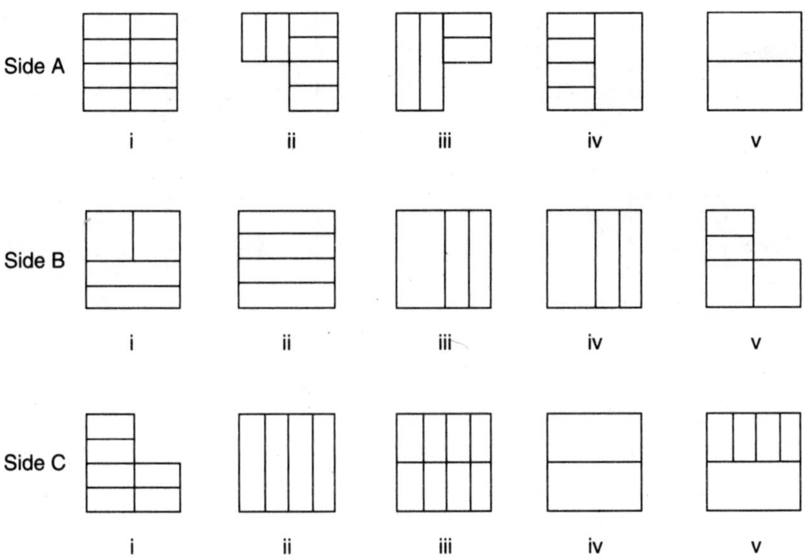
Side A
i
ii
iii
iv
v
Side B
i
ii
iii
iv
v
Side C
i
ii
iii
iv
v

6.

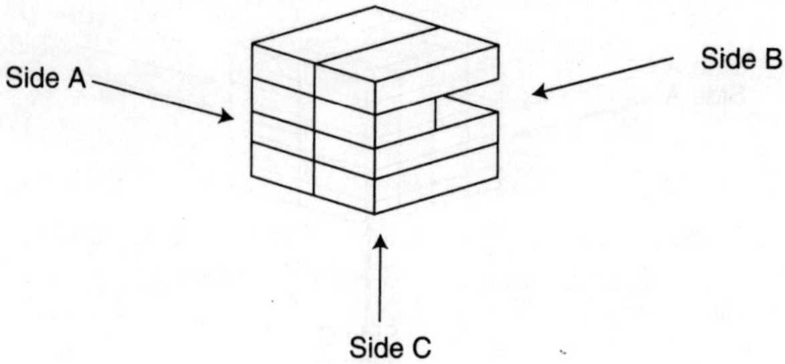

Side A

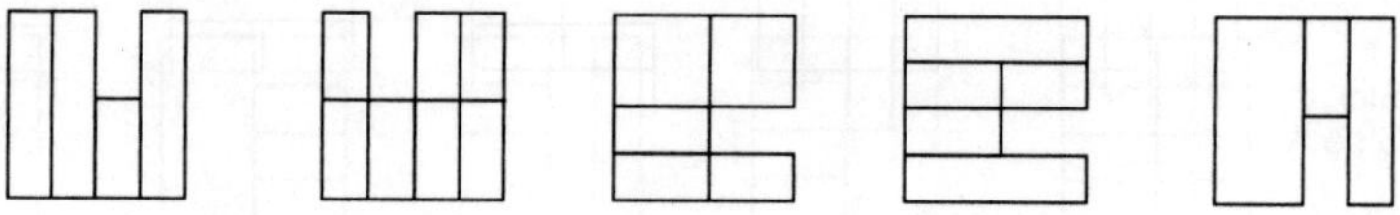

i ii iii iv v

Side B

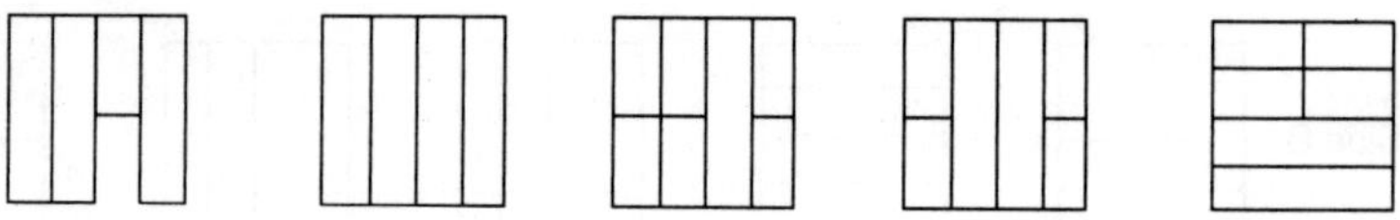

i ii iii iv v

Side C

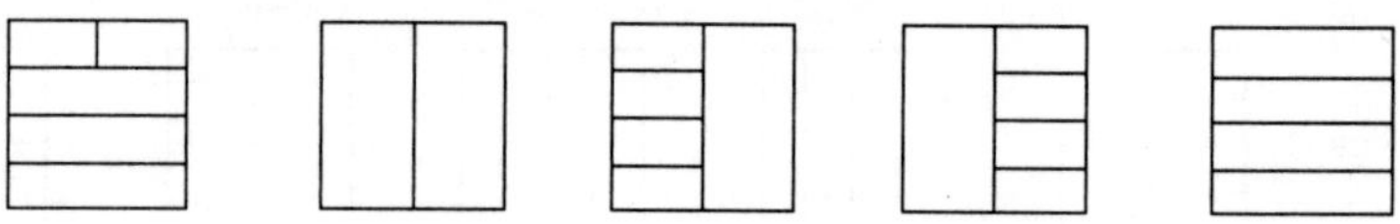

i ii iii iv v

7.

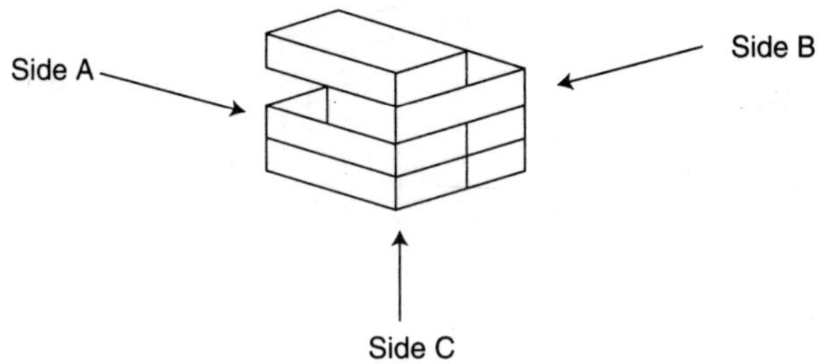
Side A
Side B
Side C

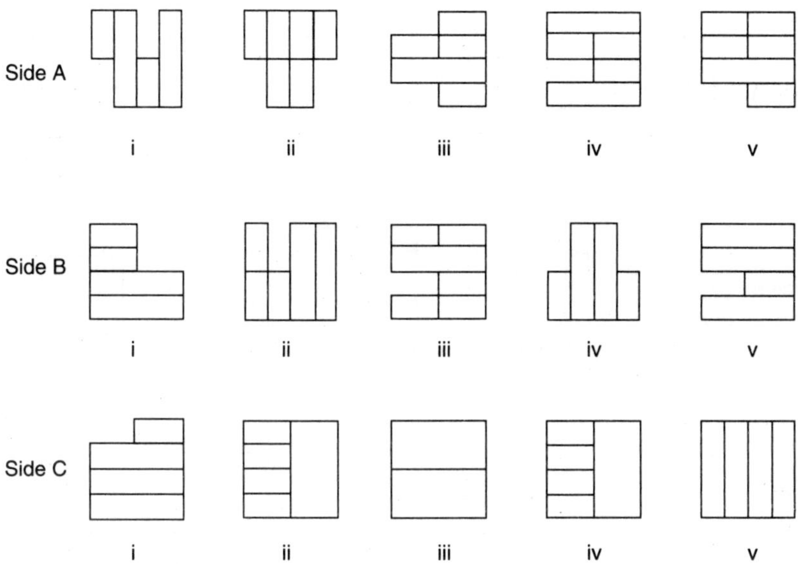
Side A
i
ii
iii
iv
v
Side B
i
ii
iii
iv
v
Side C
i
ii
iii
iv
v

8.

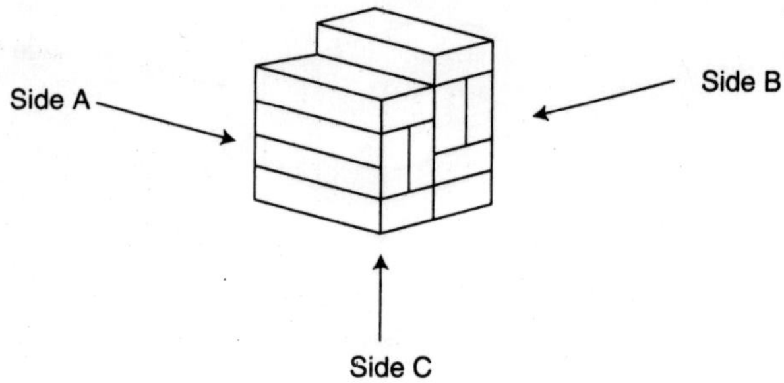
Side A
Side B
Side C

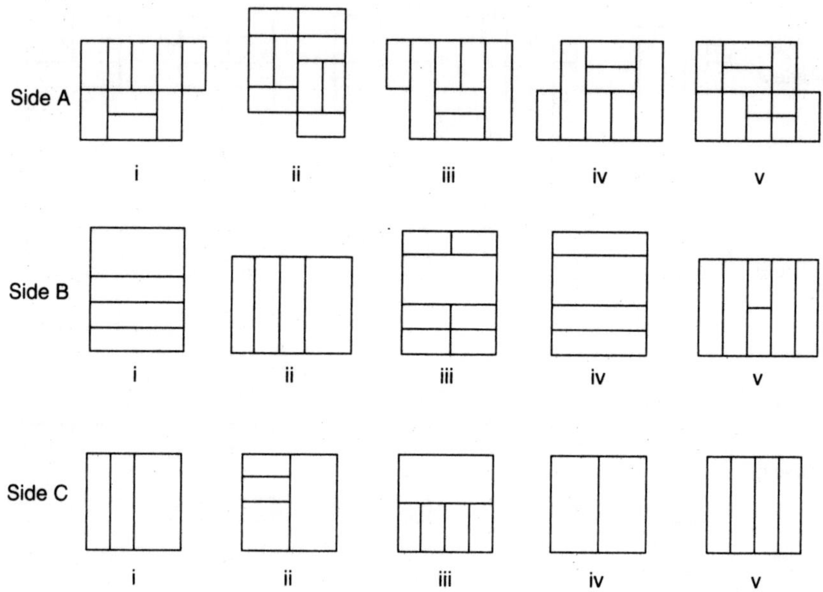
Side A
i
ii
iii
iv
v
Side B
i
ii
iii
iv
v
Side C
i
ii
iii
iv
v

9.

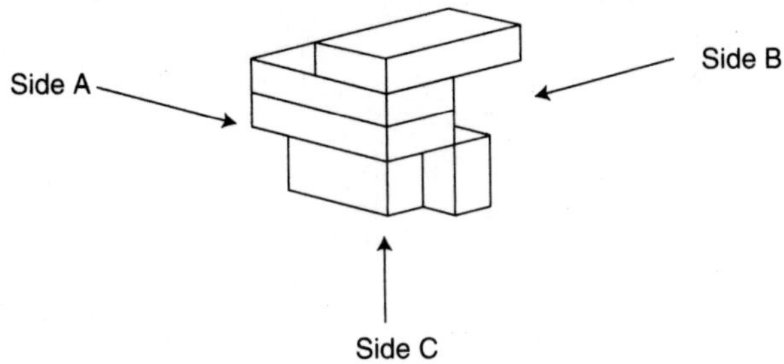

Side A

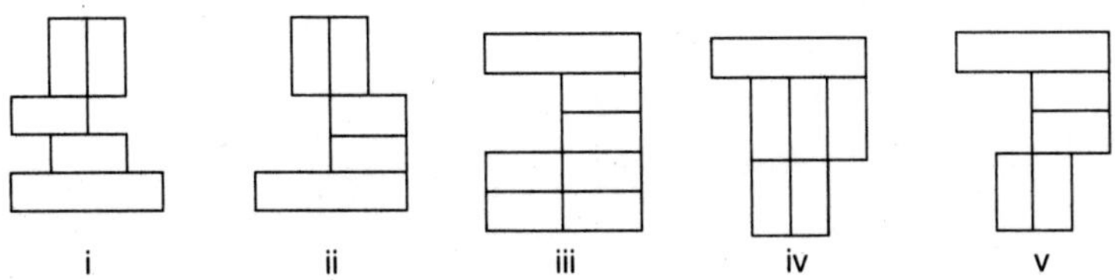

Side B

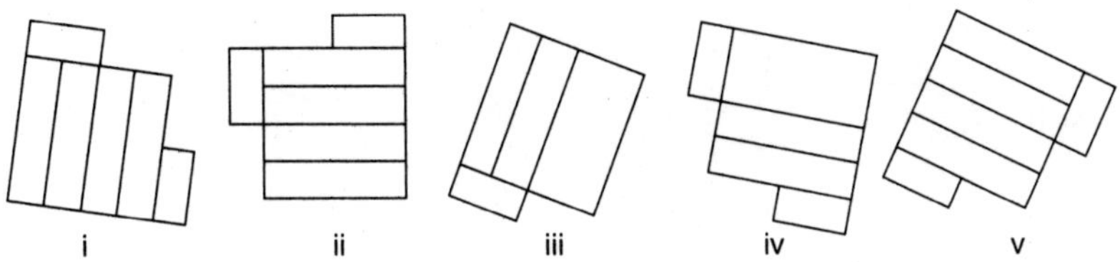

Side C

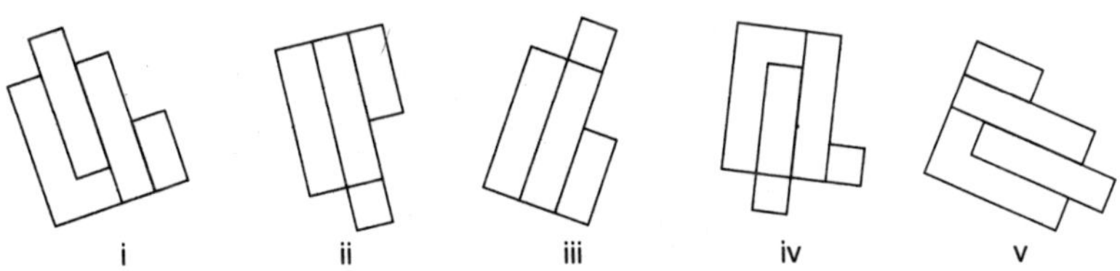

10.

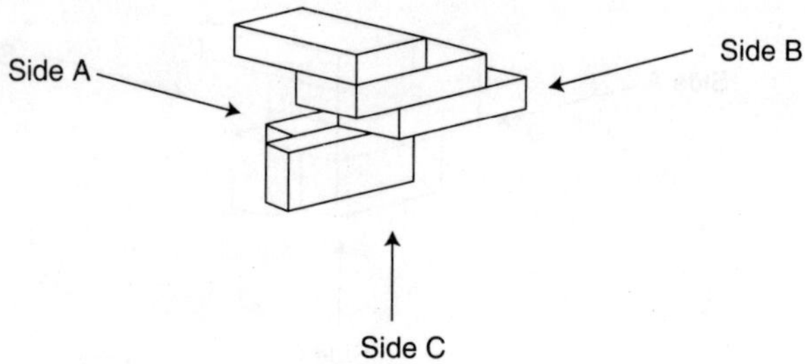
Side A
Side B
Side C

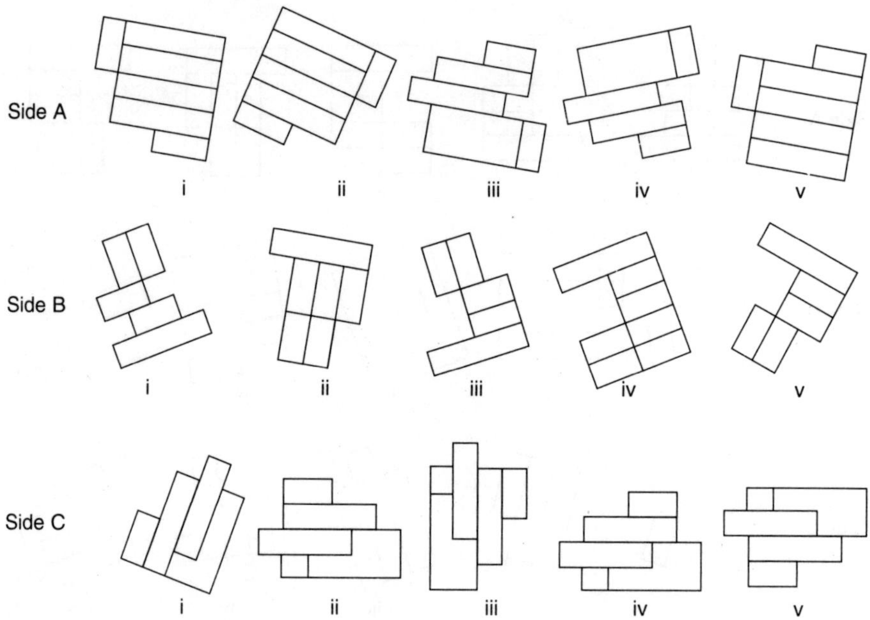
Side A
i
ii
iii
iv
v
Side B
i
ii
iii
iv
v
Side C
i
ii
iii
iv
v

Answers

1	A. iii	B. ii	C. iv
2	A. iv	B. i	C. v
3	A. iv	B. i	C. i
4	A. ii	B. iii	C. ii
5	A. iv	B. ii	C. v
6	A. i	B. iii	C. ii
7	A. v	B. v	C. iii
8	A. ii	B. iv	C. iv
9	A. v	B. iv	C. i
10	A. iii	B. iii	C. v

Scoring

Number right minus number wrong = __________

Plus 3 aged under 16, plus 2 if aged 17–20 + __________

Score on the test = __________

Use the following table to convert your test score to a score out of 10 or 'sten score'. You can then enter your 'sten score' in the chart on page 200.

Test score	1–2	3–4	5–6	7–8	9–10	11–12	13–16	17–19	20–22	23–25+
Sten score	1	2	3	4	5	6	7	8	9	10

Part 6

Practical numerical tests

This section comprises the largest number of tests, reflecting their importance and the likelihood that these are the ones that most people will encounter. You have to work with the rules of numbers: addition, subtraction, division and multiplication. It is also important to understand decimals, percentages, and fractions.

All of us use figures in relation to our personal finances and in various practical situations where calculating and estimating are a necessary part of daily life. But some people have a liking for this type of activity or a talent for it that then leads them to think of careers in which they are dealing with money, estimating or performing other arithmetical functions. The range of careers that require these skills is vast and also extremely varied.

Many people will declare that these days they leave such figure work to a calculator or to a computer and that therefore they have become 'rusty'. Nevertheless, to do well in this test requires an underlying aptitude, which will appear as an above average score, even though you may not have used the necessary skills for some time.

Test 12, Reckoning, is designed to assess your numerical agility with the basic rules of numbers. Test 13, Arithmetic, places you in a true to life office situation to see how well you can look after money transactions. Test 14, Figure work, is a wide-ranging test that stretches you on fractions and percentages as well as other number problems. Test 15, Number Skills, is even more wide ranging as it introduces measurement and asks for answers to practical problems. Test 16, Calculations, asks that you find out what is missing in a series of calculations, which involves checking that answers are correct.

In many careers, the basic calculation has to be 'summed up' quickly, even if it is a rough approximation, so that a decision can be reached in principle. This happens in many areas of financial assessment, costing, and surveying work as well as in buying and selling.

Test 12

Reckoning

You have to work out sums, using the following rules:

- \+ means plus, or add;
- – means minus, or take away;
- * means multiplied by, or times;
- / means divided by.

You *must* work out the sums in the order they are written. So, with 3+1*2/2 = ?:

First step	3+1 = 4
Second step	4*2 = 8
Third step	8/2 = 4

In the examples below, each has three sums. You have to see whether one of the sums gives an answer that is different from the other two, or whether all the answers are the same. Then you have to place a tick in the box by the correct answer. Examples 1 and 2 have been done to show you how. Work out examples 3 and 4 yourself. Mark your answer with a tick.

Example 1	☐ a) 1+2 = 3	☐ b) 3+0 = 3	☑ c) 2+2 = 4	☐ d) all the same
Example 2	☐ a) 2*2 = 4	☐ b) 3+1 = 4	☐ c) 6–2 = 4	☑ d) all the same
Example 3	☐ a) 2/2 =	☐ b) 1+1 =	☐ c) 6–4 =	☐ d) all the same
Example 4	☐ a) 2*2+1 =	☐ b) 3+1+1 =	☐ c) 4–3*2+3 =	☐ d) all the same

Check your answers for examples 3 and 4:

Example 3	☑ a) 2/2 = 1	☐ b) 1+1 = 2	☐ c) 6–4 = 2	☐ d) all the same
Example 4	☐ a) 2*2+1 =5	☐ b) 3+1+1 = 5	☐ c) 4–3*2+3 = 5	☑ d) all the same

For example 3, you should have placed a tick in the box next to a). For example 4, you should have placed your tick in the box next to d).

Do not mark this book if it is not your own, but record your answers and any working out you need to do on separate paper. If you wish to gain an estimate of your aptitude, record the number of the question you are on after exactly 8 minutes. Otherwise, take as long as you wish to complete the items.

Timed test: 8 minutes

1.	☐ a) 2+2 =	☐ b) 1+1 =	☐ c) 3+1 =	☐ d) all the same
2.	☐ a) 2+1 =	☐ b) 3+1 =	☐ c) 2+2 =	☐ d) all the same
3.	☐ a) 2+2 =	☐ b) 3+1 =	☐ c) 4+1 =	☐ d) all the same
4.	☐ a) 2–1 =	☐ b) 1+2 =	☐ c) 3–2 =	☐ d) all the same
5.	☐ a) 2 +2 =	☐ b) 1* 4 =	☐ c) 4–0 =	☐ d) all the same
6.	☐ a) 3*2 =	☐ b) 5+1 =	☐ c) 4*2 =	☐ d) all the same
7.	☐ a) 2/2 =	☐ b) 1+1 =	☐ c) 2–1 =	☐ d) all the same
8.	☐ a) 2*3 =	☐ b) 3+1+1 =	☐ c) 2+3 =	☐ d) all the same
9.	☐ a) 2/1 =	☐ b) 1+1 =	☐ c) 4/2 =	☐ d) all the same
10.	☐ a) 4*2 =	☐ b) 8/2 =	☐ c) 4–0 =	☐ d) all the same
11.	☐ a) 3/1 =	☐ b) 1+1+1 =	☐ c) 1*3 =	☐ d) all the same
12.	☐ a) 2*3 =	☐ b) 7–1 =	☐ c) 6/3 =	☐ d) all the same
13.	☐ a) 6/2 =	☐ b) 9/3 =	☐ c) 6–3 =	☐ d) all the same

	☐ a)	☐ b)	☐ c)	☐ d)
14.	2*5 =	2*2*2 =	3*2+4 =	all the same
15.	2/2*3 =	1+1*2 =	6–4*2 =	all the same
16.	2*3–2 =	3+4–2 =	10/2 =	all the same
17.	2–2+4 =	1*1+4 =	6–2 =	all the same
18.	6*2+3 =	3+1*4 =	5*2+5 =	all the same
19.	9/3*2 =	11+7/3 =	6–1*2 =	all the same
20.	2*7+2 =	2*2*2 =	1*2*4 =	all the same
21.	12/3 =	16/4 =	20/5 =	all the same
22.	20/5–2 =	36/3/6 =	27/3/3 =	all the same
23.	34/2+3 =	50/5+8 =	60/3–2 =	all the same
24.	25/5–3 =	6*3/9 =	4*5/10 =	all the same
25.	6*5/3 =	2*7–2 =	6/2+7 =	all the same
26.	9*4 =	3*12 =	4*8+6 =	all the same
27.	17*3–11 =	8*4+8 =	84/2–4 =	all the same

	☐ a)	☐ b)	☐ c)	☐ d)
28.	48/8 =	54/9 =	49/7 =	all the same
29.	101–29/6 =	87–53/2 =	77–41/3 =	all the same
30.	13*3–3 =	11*4–6 =	16*2+4 =	all the same
31.	16/2*3 =	8*6/2 =	6*4 =	all the same
32.	12*3/2 =	3*3*2 =	40/5*2 =	all the same
33.	16*3 =	5*5*2 =	24/2*4 =	all the same
34.	33/3–5 =	17+8/5 =	19–4/3 =	all the same
35.	7*9+7 =	6*11+8 =	6*9+16 =	all the same
36.	84/7/2 =	132/11–5 =	36*4/24 =	all the same
37.	116–77/13 =	16*9/48 =	93–57/12 =	all the same
38.	35/7–2 =	17*2–30 =	21–9/3 =	all the same
39.	29*3–19 =	7*14–30 =	113–79+34 =	all the same
40.	68/17 =	90/18 =	250/50 =	all the same
41.	43*4/43 =	88/11/2 =	128*3/96 =	all the same

42.	☐ a) 26+51+23/4 =	☐ b) 1000/40 =	☐ c) 55+13+32/4 =	☐ d) all the same
43.	☐ a) 898–669 =	☐ b) 108+137 =	☐ c) 1003–774 =	☐ d) all the same
44.	☐ a) 1348/337+1 =	☐ b) 687/229–1 =	☐ c) 1023/341+2 =	☐ d) all the same
45.	☐ a) 11*21–59/4 =	☐ b) 459–63/9 =	☐ c) 22*10/5 =	☐ d) all the same

Answers

1. b	11. d	21. d	31. d	41. d
2. a	12. c	22. c	32. c	42. d
3. c	13. d	23. a	33. b	43. b
4. b	14. b	24. d	34. a	44. b
5. d	15. a	25. b	35. b	45. a
6. c	16. a	26. c	36. b	
7. b	17. b	27. c	37. d	
8. a	18. b	28. c	38. a	
9. d	19. c	29. b	39. d	
10. a	20. a	30. b	40. a	

Scoring

Number right minus number wrong = __________

Plus 2 aged under 16, plus 1 if aged 17–20 + __________

Score on the test = __________

Use the following table to convert your test score to a score out of 10 or 'sten score'. You can then enter your 'sten score' in the chart on page 200.

Test score	1–17	18–20	21–24	25–26	27–28	29–30	31–33	34–35	36–38	39+
Sten score	1	2	3	4	5	6	7	8	9	10

Test 13

Arithmetic

An office keeps a box containing money (a Petty Cash Box) from which small payments can be made. In some offices, this is called a 'float'. When money is taken from the box, a note is left inside the box saying how much has been taken and what it has been taken for. These notes are written either on a Petty Cash Voucher or on a Memo.

You will be asked to do some calculations about the amounts of money that appear on the Vouchers and Memos. You are not allowed calculators or other computing aids. The Vouchers and Memos look like this:

Petty Cash Voucher

7 June

	£	p
Expenses for		
Taxi fare	10	00
Sandwiches	10	00
Total	20	00

Signature: Bob

☎ **MEMO**

I took £10 from petty cash
for stamps I put the change
– £1.00 – back in the box.

Jenny
11 June

Example questions and answers

1. How much did Jenny spend on 11 June? £9.00
2. What is £1 as a fraction (or part) of £10? 1/10
3. What percentage of Bob's voucher was spent on sandwiches? 50 per cent.

In Question 1, Jenny took £10 and put £1 back, so spent £9. In Question 2, £10 is 10 times as much as £1, so £1 is one tenth of £10. In Question 3, the total was £20 and the sandwiches cost £10, which is 50 per cent of the total.

In the test the Vouchers and Memos give information about how much money has been taken from the box. The money is taken from the box on the date of the Voucher or Memo. At the start of the test you are told how much is in the Petty Cash Box before anybody has taken anything from it.

In the test the answers you get to some of the early items will help you to work out your answers to later ones, so it is best to do the questions in the order they come. Do not mark this book if it is not your own, but record your answers and any working out you need to do on separate paper.

If you wish to gain an estimate of your aptitude, record the number of the question you are on after exactly 15 minutes. Otherwise, take as long as you wish to complete the items.

Timed test: 15 minutes

Petty Cash Voucher
7June

	£	p
Milk	4	25
Sandwiches for JH Group	8	50
Total		

Signature: Christine

Petty Cash Voucher
9 June

	£	p
Expenses for Jane Smith (interviewed 17 June)		
Train (return)	22	60
Midday snack	5	65
Total		

Signature: Sandy

Petty Cash Voucher
10 June

	£	p
Window cleaning:		
week 25th May	22	50
week 1st June	37	50
Total	60	00

Signature: Jack

Petty Cash Voucher
10 June

	£	p
Snacks on 7 June	6	72
Petrol 28 miles at 30p	2	80
Stationery items	18	48
Total	27	00

Signature: John

Petty Cash Voucher
11 June

	£	p
Stationery:		
Photocopying	5	70
Rail Guide	4	10
Stationery	7	00
Milk jug	4	20
Total		

Signature: John

Petty Cash Voucher
15 June

	£	p
Flowers for reception	8	75
Magazines for reception	6	25
Total		

Signature: Christine

Petty Cash Voucher
18 June

		£	p
Petrol expenses:			
29 May	50 miles		
1 June	20 miles		
7 June	34 miles		
16 June	96 miles		
@ 30p per mile			
Total		61	80

Signature: Bill

Petty Cash Voucher
22 June

	£	p
Travel expenses for Mr Curtis (who came for interview on 6 June)	37	00
Total	37	00

Signature: Tom

Petty Cash Voucher
22 June

	£	p
Flowers for lobby	8	70
Sandwiches for JH Group on 5 June	16	10
Taxi to station for PB	8	60
Total	28	40

Signature: Jenny

Petty Cash Voucher
23 June

	£	p
Newspapers	3	30
Magazines for lobby	7	50
Sub total	11	80
Less money not used up on taxi fare on 19 June	1	40
Total	10	40

Signature: Marty

Petty Cash Voucher 24 June		**Petty Cash Voucher** 24 June	
	£ p		£ p
Flowers for reception	15 60	Biscuits	1 86
Flowers for lobby	5 20	Sugar	1 54
Urgent stationery	10 75	Tea	2 50
		Light bulbs	3 80
Total		Batteries	2 30
Signature: Jenny		Signature: Christine	

☎ **MEMO**	☎ **MEMO**
I have taken £5 from petty cash for a taxi fare.	I took £5 from petty cash for stamps. I put the change – £1.65 – back in the box.
Marty 19 June	Jenny 11 June

Take note that a) the Petty Cash Box had £72.30 in it on 1 June; b) payments of £75 each were made into the Petty Cash Box on 6, 13, 20 and 27 June.

1. How many Vouchers and Memos are there in total?______
2. How many more Vouchers than Memos are there?______
3. What is the number of Vouchers divided by the number of Memos?______
4. What was the total of the four payments made into the Petty Cash Box?______
5. What is £75 as a percentage of the four payments made into Petty Cash?______
6. What was the total taken by Christine on 7 June?______
7. What is £4.25 as a percentage of £8.50?______
8. What was the total taken by Sandy on 9 June?______
9. What is £5.65 as a percentage of £22.60?______
10. How much more did Christine spend on flowers than magazines on 15 June?______

11. How much more did Christine spend on 15 than 24 June?______

12. What was Christine's total on 24 June as a percentage of her total on 15 June?______

13. From Jenny's Memo of 11 June, how much did she spend on stamps?______

14. How much in error was Bill's claim for petrol on 18 June?______

15. What percentage of Bill's corrected claim for petrol was his expense for 1 June?______

IMPORTANT: If you have found a voucher or memo that needed to be corrected, use the correct figures for the calculations numbers 16 to 25.

16. What was the accurate total for John's voucher on 10 June?______

17. What was John's original claim for petrol as a percentage of the correct claim?______

18. How much less did John spend on 11 June than 10 June?______

19. What were snacks as a percentage of the total of John's voucher of 10 June?______

20. What percentage of the window cleaning bill was for May?______

21. What was Jenny's correct total for 22 June?______

22. How much did Marty spend from his memo of 19 and voucher of 23 June?______

23. What percentage of the correct total for 19 and 23 June was the taxi?______

24. What was the correct amount of expense between 7 and 16 June?______

25. How much money would have remained in Petty Cash on 1 July?______

Answers

1. 14	6. £12.75	11. £3.00	16. £33.60 (or 33 1/3)	21. £33.40
2. 10	7. 50%	12. 80%	17. 33.33%	22. £14.40
3. 6 (or 1/6)	8. £28.25	13. £3.35	18. £12.60	23. 25%
4. £300	9. 25%	14. £1.80	19. 20%	24. £173.95
5. 25%	10. £2.50	15. 10%	20. 37.5%	25. £10

Scoring

Number right minus number wrong = __________

Plus 2 aged under 16, plus 1 if aged 17–20 + __________

Score on the test = __________

Use the following table to convert your test score to a score out of 10 or 'sten score'. You can then enter your 'sten score' in the chart on page 200.

Test score	1–6	7–8	9	10–11	12–13	14–15	16–17	18–19	20–21	22+
Sten score	1	2	3	4	5	6	7	8	9	10

Test 14

Figure work

In this test you are asked to work out various sums and calculations. The test involves arithmetic and will also test you on decimals, percentages and fractions. You are not allowed a calculator on this test.

In this test: '+' means add, '–' means take away or subtract, '×' means multiply or times, '/' means divide by.

For each problem write the correct answer in the space provided on the right-hand side. Look at the examples below. The first one has been done for you.

Examples

1. 10/2 = ? (Answer: 5)
2. What is 50 per cent of £20? _______
3. What is 3 × ½? _______
4. 1.3 – (minus) 0.9 = ? _______

In Example 2, the answer is £10 – 50 per cent is the same as 50 parts out of 100 or the same as five parts in 10. One part in 10 of £20 is £2, so 5 parts is £10.

In Example 3 the answer is 1½. Three half parts makes one and a half parts, which is the same as half of three.

In Example 4 the answer is 0.4. This is 13 parts take away 9 parts and then putting back the decimal point in the correct place.

Make sure you have scrap paper for any rough working you may want do on this test. Please do not mark the book if it is not your own, but record your answers on a separate sheet.

Timed test: 10 minutes

1. 10 – 5 = ? _______

2. What is 10% (10 per cent) of £40? _______

3. What is 4 × ½ (half of 4)? _______

4. 1.6 – (minus) 0.3 = ? _______

5. 21/7 = ? _______

6. What is 5% of £40? _______

7. What is 8 × ¼? _______

8. 2.1 + 1.9 = ? _______

9. 10 × 13 = ? _______

10. What is 3% of £100? _______

11. What is 16 × ¼? _______

12. 3.08 + 2.19 = ? _______

13. 156 / 12 =? _______

14. What is 1/3 × 1/3? _______

15. What is 7½% of £300? _______

16. What is 15 / 2½? _______

17. 106.7 – 103.81 = ? _______

18. What is 32/50 as a percentage? _______

19. A rectangular floor measures 2.5 metres by 3 metres. What is the size of the floor in square metres? _______

20. What is 22½% of £200? _______

21. What is 4¼ × ¼? _______

22. 0.07 × 0.02 _______

23. 17 × 29 = ? _______

24. What is 6% of £40 added to 12½% of £20? _______

25. What is 6 divided by 8? _______

26. What is 0.09 divided by 0.3? _______

27. From £50 how much change will you have if you purchase as many items as possible each costing £1.99? _______

28. How many dollars will I get for £10 if the exchange rate is 1.45 dollars to the pound? _______

29. The interest on a £1,000 loan is 20% annually. What is the total amount of interest paid at the end of year two? _______

30. If an item cost £126 when discounted to 60% of its original price what was the original price? _______

Answers

1. 5	7. 2	13. 13	19. 7.5	25. 0.75
2. £4	8. 4	14. 1/9	20. £45	26. 0.3
3. 2	9. 130	15. £22.50	21. 1 and 1/16	27. 25p
4. 1.3	10. £3	16. 6	22. 0.0014	28. £14.50
5. 3	11. 4	17. 2.89	23. 493	29. £440
6. £2	12. 5.27	18. 64%	24. £4.90	30. £210

Scoring

Number right minus number wrong = __________

Plus 2 aged under 16, plus 1 if aged 17–20 + __________

Score on the test = __________

Use the following table to convert your test score to a score out of 10 or 'sten score'. You can then enter your 'sten score' in the chart on page 200.

Test score	1–4	5–8	9–12	13–15	16–17	18–19	20–22	23–24	25–26	27+
Sten score	1	2	3	4	5	6	7	8	9	10

Test 15

Number skills

= equals, same as, for example, A=B, B=C, therefore A=C
\+ addition, plus, for example, £2.50 + £2.50 = £5.00
– subtraction, taking away, for example, £13.00 – £4.50 = £8.50
× or * multiplication, times, or by, for example, £5.00 * 3 = £15.00
/ division, dividing, for example, £12.00/4 = £3.00

This is a test of your ability to use numbers in everyday circumstances. You are given a calculation to perform. You then have to choose the correct answer from the alternatives provided for you. You are not allowed a calculator or computer. Underline or tick the correct answer. It is advisable to have a piece of scrap paper and a pencil to do any working out that may be necessary. The examples below have been done already to show you how.

Examples

1. What is £12 (twelve pounds) divided by 2?
   a) £3 b) £4 c) £12 d) £6 e) £1
2. What is 1.5 (one point five) and 0.5 (zero point 5)?
   a) 4 b) 2.5 c) 5 d) 1 e) 2
3. What is 10% (ten per cent) of 60?
   a) 1 b) 6 c) 100 d) 0 e) 40
4. What is ¼ (one quarter) of 8?
   a) 1/3 b) 4 c) 5 d) one half e) 2

The answer to Example 1 is d). There are two lots of six pounds in 12 pounds. The answer to 2 is e). 1.5 and 0.5 are ways of saying one and a half, and a half. The answer to 3 is b), since 10 per cent is the same as saying 10 parts out of a 100 or 1 part out of 10, and 60 divided by 10 is 6. The answer to 4 is e). A ¼ means 1 part in four; 8 has 2 parts of 4.

If you are timing yourself you have 10 minutes to do as much as you can. Work quickly and accurately. Remember, you are likely to need a piece of scrap paper and a pencil. Begin as soon as you are ready.

Timed test: 10 minutes

1. What is left when 5 is taken away from 17?

   a) 12 b) 16 c) 10 d) 13 e) 14

2. What is 1.5 added to 1.5?

   a) 1 b) 3 c) 3.5 d) 2 e) 2.5

3. What is 50% of £10?

   a) £2 b) £6 c) £1 d) £4 e) £5

4. What is a half plus a quarter?

   a) 1½ b) 1¾ c) ¾ d) 2 e) ¼

5. What is 6 divided by 2?

   a) 3 b) 2 c) 1/2 d) 1 e) 6

6. What is 1.25 added to 8.75?

   a) 9 b) 10 c) 11 d) 9½ e) 11

7. What is 50% of £18.50?

   a) £10.50 b) £9.25 c) £8.25 d) £9.50 e) £9

8. What is 1¾ multiplied by 2?

   a) 3 and 1/4 b) 3 and 3/4 c) 2 and 1/2 d) 2 and 3/4
   e) 3 and 1/2

9. What is 24 divided by 8?

   a) 4 b) 3 c) 5 d) 6 e) 2

10. What is 1.3 and 10.3?

    a) 10.46 b) 17.6 c) 10.43 d) 11.6 e) 10.8

11. What is 10% of £22.20?

    a) £11.10 b) £12.10 c) £2.22 d) £2.10 e) £2.20

12. What is ½ divided by 2?

    a) 1/4 b) 8 c) 2 d) 4 e) 1/2

13. What does one person get if £30 is divided among 10 people?
    a) £10 b) £2 c) £3 d) £15 e) £5

14. What is 3.6 divided by 3?
    a) 1.4 b) 1.2 c) 10.8 d) 3.2 e) 1.3

15. What is 17½% of £200?
    a) £39 b) £29 c) £70 d) £35 e) £34.50

16. What is ¾ divided by 3?
    a) 1/6 b) 1/12 c) 4 d) 1/4 e) 9

17. 16 people each receive £5. What was the total amount before the division?
    a) £70 b) £64 c) £30 d) £60 e) £80

18. What is 7.09 less 2.04?
    a) 5.05 b) 4.03 c) 5.15 d) 4.15 e) 4.05

19. What is 12½ % of £96?
    a) £18.20 b) £18 c) £14.40 d) £9.60 e) £12

20. What is a fifth of £65?
    a) £1.30 b) £13 c) £13.50 d) £12.50 e) £11

21. 7 people shared the cost of a holiday equally between them. The cost of the holiday in total was £1,785. How much did each pay?
    a) £245 b) £235 c) £265 d) £255 e) £112.20

22. What is the total of 8.001, 4.36 and 0.0098?
    a) 13.0709 b) 12.3708 c) 13.2329 d) 12.3709 e) 14.3708

23. A new car costs £18,000. How much does it cost when reduced by 5%?
    a) £17,100 b) £16,200 c) £15,000 d) £17,200 e) £17,400

24. What is 4 and a half plus 3 and five sixths?
    a) 8 and 2/3 b) 7 and 2/3 c) 9 and 2/6 d) 7 and 1/2
    e) 8 and 1/3

25. A person sold a car for £3,550, buying a new car for £16,040. What was the difference in price between the two cars?

a) £12,380 b) £12,590 c) £12,490 d) £11,490 e) £13,490

26. A length of wood measuring 1.2 metres has to be cut into three exactly equal pieces each of 285 centimetres. How many centimetres are left over?

a) 345 b) 245 c) 355 d) 145 e) 385

27. Each article costs £5.70, but a 2% reduction is given on bulk orders of 10 or more. What is the cost of 15?

a) £84.89 b) £84.79 c) £83.79 d) £83.69 e) £73.79

28. What is one seventh of one seventh?

a) 49 b) 1/49 c) 1/7 d) 7 e) 1/14

29. A restaurant bill for two people was £36.30. One person's meal was exactly twice as much as the other's. What was the cost of the cheaper meal?

a) £13.10 b) £26.20 c) £12.15 d) £12.10 e) £12.20

30. The cost of apples is £1.80 per kilo. When the apples weigh 2.8 kilos, what is the total cost?

a) £4 b) £4.84 c) £4.94 d) £5.14 e) £5.04

31. Four children out of a class of 25 were not able to read. What percentage is this?

a) 25% b) 16% c) 12% d) 8% e) 15%

32. What is 2/5 added to 1/6 and 1/3?

a) 7/8 b) 17/18 c) 29/30 d) 4/5 e) 9/10

33. A group of 8 adults and 16 children paid a total of £5,400 for a holiday. The cost per adult was twice that of each child. What was the cost per child?

a) £540 b) £270 c) £225 d) £168.75 e) £337.50

34. What is 3.073 divided by 0.04?

a) 76.825 b) 7.6825 c) 768.25 d) 7682.5 e) 0.76825

35. What is 27% of £425?

a) £94.75 b) £114.75 c) £104.75 d) £124.75 e) £84.75

36. What is 3/16 of 200 written as a percentage?

a) 62.5% b) 77.5% c) 75% d) 65% e) 37.5%

37. What is 1,095 multiplied by 13 and divided by 15?

a) 949 b) 1049 c) 948 d) 959 e) 947

38. What is 0.07 divided by 350?

a) 0.2 b) 0.02 c) 0.002 d) 0.0002 e) 2

39. By the time a man decided to buy a house the cost had inflated by around 8 % to £182,000. What was the approximate price before inflation?

a) £170,000 b) £167,500 c) £168,500 d) £169,000
e) £159,500

40. What is 3 and 1/2 divided by 2 and 1/4?

a) 6 and 1/8 b) 1 and 1/2 c) 1 and 8/9 d) 1 and 4/5
e)1 and 5/9

Answers

1. a	6. b	11. c	16. d	21. d	26. a	31. b	36. c
2. b	7. b	12. a	17. e	22. b	27. c	32. e	37. a
3. e	8. e	13. c	18. a	23.a	28. b	33. d	38. d
4. c	9. b	14. b	19. e	24. e	29. d	34. a	39. c
5. a	10. d	15. d	20. b	25. c	30. e	35. b	40. e

Scoring

Number right minus number wrong = __________

Plus 2 aged under 16, plus 1 if aged 17–20 + __________

Score on the test = __________

Use the following table to convert your test score to a score out of 10 or 'sten score'. You can then enter your 'sten score' in the chart on page 200.

Test score	1–2	3–4	5–8	9–12	13–16	17–20	21–25	26–30	31–35	36+
Sten score	1	2	3	4	5	6	7	8	9	10

Test 16

Calculations

In this test you are given a sum from which you have to work out the figure that is missing. You have to choose the correct answer from the five alternatives provided. (Remember that + means add, – means take away, * means multiply and / means divide.)

You can mark your answer on the page in the way that suits you best. You can cross the correct answer through, mark with a tick, circle or underline. It is best to mark your answer with a pencil so that you can erase it if you change your mind. Have some spare paper available in case you need it for any rough work. Examples 1 and 2 below have been done already.

Examples – what is the missing figure?

1. 9/3 = ?	3	4	9	527	
a	b	c	d	e	
2. 12 * ? = 24	7	24	2	86	
a	b	c	d	e	
3. £5.00/2 = ?	£.5	£1	£2.50	£1.50	£10
	a	b	c	d	e

4. £1.50 + £2.00 +? = £6.00	£2	£1.50	£1	£2.50	£0.50
	a	b	c	d	e

In the first example the number 9 divided by 3 gives 3. In the second example 12 is multiplied by 2 to give 24. In the third example £5.00 divided by 2 gives £2.50. In the fourth example £2.50 has to be added to £1.50 and £2.00 to make £6.00.

This test lasts 12 minutes. You have to work accurately and do as many questions as you can in the time allowed. When you are ready, turn over the page and start your timer as you do so.

Timed test: 12 minutes

What is the missing figure?

1. 6 + 9 = ?

14	15	3	17	18
a	b	c	d	e

2. 11 + ? = 23

12	14	6	10	11
a	b	c	d	e

3. ? – 4 = 3

8	1	7	9	6
a	b	c	d	e

4. 12/2 = ?

1	8	4	24	6
a	b	c	d	e

5. ?/8 = 2

16	4	12	2	8
a	b	c	d	e

6. 5 * ? = 35

3	9	6	7	5
a	b	c	d	e

7. 15 + ? + 15 = 40

24	5	20	10	15
a	b	c	d	e

8. 16 * ? = 48

2	32	8	4	3
a	b	c	d	e

9. 35 – ? = 19

16	21	26	54	70
a	b	c	d	e

10. ?/7 = 13

81	19	13	91	61
a	b	c	d	e

11. 38 * 7 = ?

196	166	266	264	164
a	b	c	d	e

12. ? – 94 = 167

198	261	241	291	271
a	b	c	d	e

13. £6.50 + ? = £10

£2.50	£4.50	£1.50	£2.00	£3.50
a	b	c	d	e

14. £9.75 – ? = £5.95

£1.80	£3.80	£1.90	£3.20	£4.20
a	b	c	d	e

15. ? * 9 = 216

24	23	14	34	22
a	b	c	d	e

16. 217 + 318 + ? = 1006

371	605	535	471	392
a	b	c	d	e

17. 39 * ? = 351

12	8	9	10	11
a	b	c	d	e

18. 1091 – ? = 892

199	99	209	189	210
a	b	c	d	e

19. 7.5/3 = ?

22.5	21.5	2.5	3.5	2.00
a	b	c	d	e

20. 4.9 * ? = 29.4

6.1	5.5	2.5	7	6
a	b	c	d	e

21. 51.2 + 38.9 + ? = 101.5

22.8	11.4	10.6	11.2	12.4
a	b	c	d	e

22. £13.91 – ? = £9.64

£4.23	£4.33	£5.27	£3.27	£4.27
a	b	c	d	e

23. ? * 10.5 = 210

20.5	40	30	20	15
a	b	c	d	e

24. ?/4 = £11.05

£44.2	£28.2	£40.2	£45	£46
a	b	c	d	e

25. £20 * 10% = ?

£1	£10	£0.2	£2	£2.2
a	b	c	d	e

26. £24.5 + ? + 107.77 = £299.81

£167.54	£268.67	£168.64	£167.2	£158.94
a	b	c	d	e

27. ? * 25% = £37.5

£115	£150	£75	£18.75	£75
a	b	c	d	e

28. ? * 7.3 = 424.13

57.1	57.9	58.1	59.1	56.1
a	b	c	d	e

29. £76 * 15 = ?

£980	£1040	£1220	£1340	£1140
a	b	c	d	e

30. ?/11 = £114.6

£1060.4	£1160.4	£1260.6	£1140.6	£1160.6
a	b	c	d	e

31. £151.91 + £263.87 + £23.99 = ?

£429.77	£439.77	£429.87	£429.77	£439.87
a	b	c	d	e

Answers

1. b	6. d	11. c	16. d	21. b	26. a
2. a	7. d	12. b	17. c	22. e	27. b
3. c	8. e	13. e	18. a	23. d	28. c
4. e	9. a	14. b	19. c	24. a	29. e
5. a	10. d	15. a	20. e	25. d	30. c
					31. b

Scoring

Number right minus number wrong = __________

Plus 2 aged under 16, plus 1 if aged 17–20 + __________

Score on the test = __________

Use the following table to convert your test score to a score out of 10 or 'sten score'. You can then enter your 'sten score' in the chart on page 200.

Test score	1–3	4	5–6	7–8	9–10	11–12	13–14	15–17	18–21	22+
Sten score	1	2	3	4	5	6	7	8	9	10

Part 7

System tests

Both tests in this section are demanding of your aptitude for quick decision making whilst maintaining absolute concentration. Accuracy is essential. The process mirrors what happens in many forms of programming and operations work where once an error slips in, it becomes difficult, time-consuming and costly to go back and 'unearth' the problem. Thus, the approach you take to these tests can be revealing. For example, even though you may get a high score because of your natural intelligence, psychologists will look carefully at whether you also made a lot of errors, as this may count against you for some tasks where accuracy, though slow, is preferable to quantity that is unreliable.

Test 17, Systems, assesses your effectiveness in converting one set of data into another. Most people check off one symbol at a time as they appear and this is a good way to establish accuracy and organization because the occasional error, even if it does appear, is not likely to appear again. This is not always the case when a person memorizes the symbol and its letter; whilst quicker, any error can get built into the process so that a whole sequence of errors can arise. An advantage of the memorization approach is that it can help with 'problem resolution' where errors may be discovered by scanning the process rather than checking each item individually.

The same remarks are relevant to Test 18, Coding, although this test is different in that the answer is always new and will always make recognizable sense. However, even if the answer may be guessed part way through the problem-solving process, it still has to be confirmed.

The aptitudes measured in this section are desirable in careers involving financial transactions, legal work and many areas of administration. This type of aptitude, especially as revealed by Test 18, is also demanded in computer programming, analysis and web design.

Test 17

Systems

In this test you are given a series and letters and symbols in a row. Each letter goes with a particular symbol. The letter is in the top box of each pair and the symbol is at the bottom.

Your task is to write in the letter that goes with each symbol. The example below shows you how. The first nine boxes in the example have been done already. Complete the last three yourself.

Example

A	B	C	D	E	F	G	H	I	J	K	L
✈	⌖	☜	🕯	❄	✡	✞	✋	⚐	💣	☯	☪

Example answer

D	G	J	H	D	F	A	K	I			
🕯	✞	💣	✋	🕯	✡	✈	☯	⚐	☜	✈	⌖

The answers to 10, 11 and 12 are C, A and B.

For each row of letters and symbols, look at each symbol and the letter above it. Then write in the missing letter that goes with each symbol for each of the test items. It is important to do this as quickly as possible without making mistakes.

Do not mark this book if it is not your own, but record your answers and any working out you need to do on separate paper. If you wish to gain an estimate of your aptitude, record the number of the question you are on after exactly 4 minutes. Otherwise, take as long as you wish to complete the items.

Timed test: 4 minutes

A	B	C	D	E	F	G	H	I	J	K	L
✈	⌖	☜	🕯	❄	✡	✞	✋	🏳	💣	☯	☪

1	2	3	4	5	6	7	8	9	10	11	12
☪	✈	💣	✋	🏳	❄	✈	✋	☪	⌖	✈	🕯

13	14	15	16	17	18	19	20	21	22	23	24
🏳	✋	🕯	☪	🏳	✡	☪	☜	🏳	⌖	❄	✡

25	26	27	28	29	30	31	32	33	34	35	36
☪	☯	☜	✡	☪	✈	🏳	❄	✞	✋	💣	✈

37	38	39	40	41	42	43	44	45	46	47	48
✡	💣	✞	☪	🕯	⌖	☯	💣	❄	✡	🕯	☜

49	50	51	52	53	54	55	56	57	58	59	60
☯	❄	🏳	🕯	☯	✡	✈	☜	✞	☪	💣	✞

A	B	C	D	E	F	G	H	I	J	K	L
✈	⌖	☜	🕯	❄	✡	✝	✋	⚐	💣	☯	☪

61	62	63	64	65	66	67	68	69	70	71	72
✝	✡	✋	☯	☯	⌖	💣	🕯	☪	✝	✈	☜

73	74	75	76	77	78	79	80	81	82	83	84
🕯	✋	✝	⚐	⌖	☪	☯	❄	☪	⚐	✡	🕯

85	86	87	88	89	90	91	92	93	94	95	96
✡	💣	✈	✋	☪	☯	❄	✈	⌖	✋	🕯	✝

97	98	99	100	101	102	103	104	105	106	107	108
✋	✡	⚐	⌖	☪	🕯	⚐	☪	✈	⌖	💣	✋

109	110	111	112	113	114	115	116	117	118	119	120
☯	💣	⌖	✈	✝	⚐	❄	💣	✋	✡	🕯	✝

A	B	C	D	E	F	G	H	I	J	K	L
✈	⌖	☞	🕯	❄	✡	✞	✋	⚐	💣	☯	☪

M	N	O	P	Q	R	S	T	U	V	W	X
❖	♌	■	●	&	♒	♎	♋	📫	♓	⍓	◆

121	122	123	124	125	126	127	128	129	130	131	132
☞	⚐	💣	☯	☪	♋	📫	♓	⍓	◆	✈	⌖

133	134	135	136	137	138	139	140	141	142	143	144
&	✡	✞	■	✋	⚐	💣	☯	☪	♌	✞	♒

145	146	147	148	149	150	151	152	153	154	155	156
♋	📫	♓	◆	☪	♎	🕯	❄	📫	☞	&	❖

157	158	159	160	161	162	163	164	165	166	167	168
♌	♒	✈	✈	⌖	📫	&	☞	❖	◆	■	💣

A	B	C	D	E	F	G	H	I	J	K	L
✈	🕈	☜	🕯	❄	✡	✞	✋	🏳	💣	☯	☪

M	N	O	P	Q	R	S	T	U	V	W	X
❖	♌	■	●	&	♒	♎	♋	📪	♓	⍓	◆

169	170	171	172	173	174	175	176	177	178	179	180
&	☪	♒	📪	♌	&	■	🏳	💣	✡	✋	♎

181	182	183	184	185	186	187	188	189	190	191	192
◆	✡	✞	✋	■	✈	☪	🕯	❄	&	❖	☜

193	194	195	196	197	198	199	200	201	202	203	204
📪	♌	♎	☜	❖	☪	◆	♒	✋	🏳	💣	■

205	206	207	208	209	210	211	212	213	214	215	216
◆	❖	☜	📪	♎	✈	☜	🕯	☪	🕯	❄	♒

Answers

It is rare for people who have approached this test seriously to have made more than an occasional error, so the number of items you have attempted will provide an overall reliable score. If you think you have been guessing you should check your answers and, after allowing yourself two errors, take away any more errors from the number attempted.

Scoring

Number right minus number wrong = __________ (if more than 3 errors)

Use the following table to convert your test score to a score out of 10 or 'sten score'. You can then enter your 'sten score' in the chart on page 200.

Test score	1–10	11–25	26–40	41–55	56–70	71–90	91–110	111–130	131–149	150+
Sten score	1	2	3	4	5	6	7	8	9	10

Test 18

Coding

This is a test of how quickly you can form the correct word from drawings or symbols. You are given a line of symbols from which you have to work out the correct word making use of a chart. You have to write in the correct word in the space provided.

It is best to mark your answer with a pencil so that you can erase it if you change your mind. Examples 1 and 2 below have been done already.

Chart

4	5	6	0	=	Θ	E	P	O	[	Σ	Γ	ϑ
A	B	C	D	E	F	G	H	I	J	K	L	M
Λ	ϵ	∴	Ξ	ζ	N	1	φ	–	λ	α	γ	M
N	O	P	Q	R	S	T	U	V	W	X	Y	Z

Examples

1. Θ46 = FACE
2. γϵφ YOU
3. NO1 ______
4. 4Oζ ______

In the third example the answer is SIT and in the fourth example the answer is AIR.

This test lasts 6 minutes. You have to work accurately and do as many as you can in the time allowed. Do not mark this book if it is not your own, but record your answers and any working out you need to do on separate paper. If you wish to gain an estimate of your aptitude, record the number of the question you are on after exactly 6 minutes. Otherwise, take as long as you wish to complete the items.

Timed test: 6 minutes

Chart

4	5	6	0	=	Θ	E	P	O	[	Σ	Γ	ϑ
A	B	C	D	E	F	G	H	I	J	K	L	M
Λ	ϵ	∴	Ξ	ζ	N	1	φ	–	ι	α	γ	M
N	O	P	Q	R	S	T	U	V	W	X	Y	Z

1. 400 ____________
2. Eϵ ____________
3. 5ϵι ____________
4. 6ζγ ____________
5. 0O∴ ____________
6. ΘO5 ____________
7. E4∴ ____________
8. ϑOα ____________
9. ∴4γ ____________
10. MO∴ ____________

4	5	6	0	=	Θ	E	P	O	[	Σ	Γ	ϑ
A	B	C	D	E	F	G	H	I	J	K	L	M
Λ	ϵ	∴	Ξ	ζ	N	1	φ	–	ι	α	γ	M
N	O	P	Q	R	S	T	U	V	W	X	Y	Z

11. ιOΓ0 ____________

12. φEΓγ ____________

13. 14ΓΣ ____________

14. ζ4–= ____________

15. ∴ζϵ0 ____________

16. ΞφO∴ ____________

17. O0ϵΓ ____________

18. E4ιΣ ____________

19. 0=Λ1 ____________

20. Eζ=γ ____________

4	5	6	0	=	Θ	E	P	O	[	Σ	Γ	ϑ
A	B	C	D	E	F	G	H	I	J	K	L	M
Λ	ϵ	∴	Ξ	ζ	N	1	φ	–	ι	α	γ	M
N	O	P	Q	R	S	T	U	V	W	X	Y	Z

21. =αOΓ= ____________

22. ∴ζOM= ____________

23. ΘΓφNP ____________

24. ϑϵζ14Γ ____________

25. Pφϑ5Γγ ____________

26. 0ON64ζ0 ____________

27. 0=ΛOM=Λ ____________

28. OΛNφζ= ____________

29. ΘφN6ϵφN ____________

30. N4Γϑ4EφΛ0O ____________

Answers

1. ADD	11. WILD	21. EXILE
2. GO	12. UGLY	22. PRIZE
3. BOW	13. TALK	23. FLUSH
4. CRY	14. RAVE	24. MORTAL
5. DIP	15. PROD	25. HUMBLY
6. FIB	16. QUIP	26. DISCARD
7. GAP	17. IDOL	27. DENIZEN
8. MIX	18. GAWK	28. INSURE
9. PAY	19. DENT	29. FUSCOUS
10. ZIP	20. GREY	30. SALMAGUNDI

Grades

A score of 23 or over grade	A
18–22	B
14–17	C
9–13	D
5–8	E
0–4	F

Scoring

Number right minus number wrong = __________

Plus 2 aged under 16, plus 1 if aged 17–20 + __________

Score on the test = __________

Use the following table to convert your test score to a score out of 10 or 'sten score'. You can then enter your 'sten score' in the chart on page 200.

Test score	1–3	4–5	6–7	8–9	10–12	13–15	16–17	18–19	20–21	22+
Sten score	1	2	3	4	5	6	7	8	9	10

Part 8

Practical verbal tests

All three tests in this section seek to assess your ability to use the English language effectively. Basic skills are, quite rightly, necessary for many jobs, so spelling is an essential. This is not always a requirement, however, where comprehension may be the important thing. In this case, the tests are measuring more abstract potential for reasoning with the meanings of words. This is a requirement in many careers, especially high-level, professional and managerial ones, where understanding the implications of what is being said or written, together with any innuendo, is essential. Language tests are often the most complex, because a word may be used in many different ways. Words are 'slippery', having alternative, deeper or hidden meanings.

Test 19, Word Usage, is a test of comprehension and spelling, and how well you understand words. Test 20, Vocabulary, deliberately stretches your vocabulary. It is the type of test that may be given to 'high flyers' who are applying for executive administrative positions. In Test 21, Verbal Precision, vocabulary is again important as an excellent indication of your potential for reasoning with words. Clearly, your level and type of education are important here, so that English graduates, who have studied the language and its literature intensely, would be expected to achieve above average results.

If you do well in these tests there are many careers available to you, particularly in areas where written communication is important, such as journalism, public relations, advertising and administrative roles.

Test 19

Word usage

In this test you are asked to choose the correct word from those given. You have to tick the box under the correct word. Look at the examples below. Examples 1 and 2 have been done to show you how. Answer the other examples for yourself by placing a tick in the correct box.

Example 1

A piano is a large, musical ____________ . Which word should go in the missing space?

country	instrument	ship	band	animal
☐ a)	☐ b)	☐ c)	☐ d)	☐ e)

Example 2

Which word has the incorrect spelling?

national	comment	bargain	certan	friend
☐ a)	☐ b)	☐ c)	☐ d)	☐ e)

Example 3

Which word is the odd one out?

argue	clash	agree	fight	dispute
☐ a)	☐ b)	☐ c)	☐ d)	☐ e)

Example 4

What is the second word in this jumbled sentence when it is in the proper order?

machine	a	is	helicopter	flying
☐ a)	☐ b)	☐ c)	☐ d)	☐ e)

In Example 2, the correct spelling is 'certain'. In Example 3, the odd one out is 'agree'. All the other words are about 'disagreement'. In Example 4, the correct order for the sentence is: 'A helicopter is a flying machine.' The second word is 'helicopter'. (Although it is possible to have other sentences: 'A flying machine is a helicopter' or 'A machine is a flying helicopter' neither of these is as sensible as: 'A helicopter is a flying machine.')

Do not mark this book if it is not your own, but record your answers and any working out you need to do on separate paper. If you wish to gain an estimate of your aptitude, record the number of the question you are on after exactly 8 minutes. Otherwise, take as long as you wish to complete the items.

Timed test: 8 minutes

1. Cycling is a ________. Which word goes in the missing space?

wheel	sport	window	machine	fish
☐ a)	☐ b)	☐ c)	☐ d)	☐ e)

2. Which word has the incorrect spelling?

traveling	offering	fastened	forbidden	apply
☐ a)	☐ b)	☐ c)	☐ d)	☐ e)

3. Which word is the odd one out?

correct	genuine	real	untrue	honest
☐ a)	☐ b)	☐ c)	☐ d)	☐ e)

4. If the first word is 'Biology' what is the second word?

life the science of is biology.

the	science	is	of	life
☐ a)	☐ b)	☐ c)	☐ d)	☐ e)

5. First aid is help given to an ___– person.

unhelpful	intoxicated	unqualified	injured	impoverished
☐ a)	☐ b)	☐ c)	☐ d)	☐ e)

6. Which word has the incorrect spelling?

lonely	rebellious	february	misprint	adress
☐ a)	☐ b)	☐ c)	☐ d)	☐ e)

7. Which word is the odd one out?

drop	hasten	surge	spring	rush
☐ a)	☐ b)	☐ c)	☐ d)	☐ e)

8. What is the first word in this jumbled sentence when it is in the proper order?

Cuba for is famous tobacco.

famous	Cuba	is	tobacco	for
☐ a)	☐ b)	☐ c)	☐ d)	☐ e)

9. Pipelines can __- water or oil over great distances.

roll	pull	lift	push	carry
☐ a)	☐ b)	☐ c)	☐ d)	☐ e)

10. Which word has the incorrect spelling?

drinkible	legible	permissible	contemptible	sociable
☐ a)	☐ b)	☐ c)	☐ d)	☐ e)

11. Which word is the odd one out?

indifferent	casual	mindful	careless	neglectful
☐ a)	☐ b)	☐ c)	☐ d)	☐ e)

12. What is the first word in this jumbled sentence when it is in the proper order?

    of Italy consists a and islands peninsula.

consists	islands	peninsula	of	Italy
☐ a)	☐ b)	☐ c)	☐ d)	☐ e)

13. A formula is a set form of words or symbols in which something is ___.

used	defined	recommended	corrected	concealed
☐ a)	☐ b)	☐ c)	☐ d)	☐ e)

14. Which word has the incorrect spelling?

paralysis	negociate	embarrass	questionable	immediately
☐ a)	☐ b)	☐ c)	☐ d)	☐ e)

15. Which word is the odd one out?

incompatible	contrasted	unequal	similar	diverse
☐ a)	☐ b)	☐ c)	☐ d)	☐ e)

16. If the last word is 'sun,' what is the third word when these words make a proper sentence?

    a sun revolves planet the round.

revolves	a	round	planet	the
☐ a)	☐ b)	☐ c)	☐ d)	☐ e)

17. Breathing ___ allows people to work in a poisoned atmosphere.

involuntarily	mechanically	apparatus	harness	intermittently
☐ a)	☐ b)	☐ c)	☐ d)	☐ e)

18. Which word has the incorrect spelling?

breathe	secretery	delinquent	tolerant	receipt
☐ a)	☐ b)	☐ c)	☐ d)	☐ e)

19. Which word is the odd one out?

burnish	lustre	tarnish	polish	shine
☐ a)	☐ b)	☐ c)	☐ d)	☐ e)

20. What is the second word in this jumbled sentence when it is in the proper order?

business an sound efficient is financially.

financially	efficient	is	an	sound
☐ a)	☐ b)	☐ c)	☐ d)	☐ e)

21. Bacteria can ____ food and spread disease.

analyse	cover	sanitise	eliminate	contaminate
☐ a)	☐ b)	☐ c)	☐ d)	☐ e)

22. Which word has the incorrect spelling?

observant	implement	repellent	environment	committment
☐ a)	☐ b)	☐ c)	☐ d)	☐ e)

23. Which word is the odd one out?

rebellious	amenable	tame	cultivated	ordered
☐ a)	☐ b)	☐ c)	☐ d)	☐ e)

24. If the first word is 'Plastics,' what is the sixth word when the following words make a sentence?

plastics heat and pressure are materials moulded by that are.

heat	are	moulded	pressure	materials
☐ a)	☐ b)	☐ c)	☐ d)	☐ e)

25. In engineering, a ___ is a movable piece which stops or allows the passage of fluid.

clock	meter	switch	valve	gauge
☐ a)	☐ b)	☐ c)	☐ d)	☐ e)

26. Which word has the incorrect spelling?

accomplish	assignment	consultant	tasteful	qoverment
☐ a)	☐ b)	☐ c)	☐ d)	☐ e)

27. Which word is the odd one out?

mock	artificial	genuine	assumed	fictitious
☐ a)	☐ b)	☐ c)	☐ d)	☐ e)

28. If the first word is 'The,' what is the eighth word when these words make a proper sentence?

    the word is a describe to state perfection of Utopia.

perfection	state	Utopia	things	word
☐ a)	☐ b)	☐ c)	☐ d)	☐ e)

29. The number of times an event happens at regular intervals is called its ___.

fibrillation	waves	average	frequency	timing
☐ a)	☐ b)	☐ c)	☐ d)	☐ e)

30. Which word has the incorrect spelling?

corrupt	managable	depressing	unnerving	consensus
☐ a)	☐ b)	☐ c)	☐ d)	☐ e)

31. Which word is the odd one out?

patronise	endorse	impugn	espouse	defend
☐ a)	☐ b)	☐ c)	☐ d)	☐ e)

32. What is the last word in this jumbled sentence when it is in the proper order?

    shells fossils and bones include animals of.

fossils	of	include	animals	shells
☐ a)	☐ b)	☐ c)	☐ d)	☐ e)

33. The ubiquitous spirit worshipped by the Incas thus ___ everything.

destroyed	invaded	pervaded	owned	idolised
☐ a)	☐ b)	☐ c)	☐ d)	☐ e)

34. Which word has the incorrect spelling?

opening	unnecesarily	grievously	openness	benefited
☐ a)	☐ b)	☐ c)	☐ d)	☐ e)

35. Which word is the odd one out?

virtuoso	wizard	maestro	prodigy	disciple
☐ a)	☐ b)	☐ c)	☐ d)	☐ e)

36. What is the last word in this jumbled sentence when it is in the proper order?

    depends the upon factors from distance sea climate such as.

climate	factor	depends	sea	distance
☐ a)	☐ b)	☐ c)	☐ d)	☐ e)

Answers

1. b	10. a	19. c	28. a
2. a	11. c	20. b	29. d
3. d	12. e	21. e	30. b
4. c	13. b	22. e	31. c
5. d	14. b	23. a	32. d
6. e	15. d	24. c	33. c
7. a	16. a	25. d	34. b
8. b	17. c	26. e	35. e
9. e	18. b	27. c	36. d

Scoring

Number right minus number wrong = __________

Plus 4 aged under 16, plus 2 if aged 17–20 + __________

Score on the test = __________

Use the following table to convert your test score to a score out of 10 or 'sten score'. You can then enter your 'sten score' in the chart on page 200.

Test score	1–8	9	10–12	13–15	16–18	19–21	22–24	25–27	28–30	31+
Sten score	1	2	3	4	5	6	7	8	9	10

Test 20

Vocabulary

This is a test of your understanding of words. You are given a word and have to say which one of the alternatives is closest in meaning to it. You have to place a tick in the correct box. Look at the examples below.

Examples

1) OWN	2) ADD
☐ a) possess	☐ a) subtract
☐ b) unpaid	☐ b) count
☐ c) disown	☐ c) duke
☐ d) landlord	☐ d) new

In Example 1, to 'possess' means the same as to 'own'. If you think of a sentence with the word own in, you will find that the word possess could replace it. For example, 'I own a car – I possess a car.' 'Unpaid' means 'owing', not to 'own'. 'Disown' means the opposite of to 'own'. Landlord means an 'owner', not to 'own'. 'Own' and 'possess' are verbs, whilst 'unpaid' is an adjective; 'disown' is a verb, but means the opposite of 'own', and 'landlord' is a noun.

In Example 2, 'subtract' is the opposite of 'add', although it is a verb, as 'add' is a verb. 'Duke' is a noun, but does not mean 'add'. 'New' means 'fresh', and therefore could be added, but it would not be able to replace the word 'add' in a sentence. In any case, 'fresh' is an adjective. Both 'add' and 'count' are verbs. 'Count' is the answer, because it is almost identical in meaning to 'add' and could easily replace it in a sentence, for example, 'You should *add* up your money –You should *count* up your money.' It does not matter that 'count' can have other meanings, for example, as a noun in 'The count and countess were invited to the Palace.'

You can do the items in any order you like, although the questions get increasingly difficult. Do not mark this book if it is not your own, but record your answers and any working out you need to do on separate paper. If you wish to gain an estimate of your aptitude, record the number of the question you are on after exactly 5 minutes. Otherwise, You can have as much time as you want to do this test, but it is probably not worth spending any longer than 5 minutes, as you will find that you either know the meanings of the words, or you do not.

Timed test: 5 minutes

Place a tick in the box of the alternative that is closest in meaning to the word in capitals.

1) BAD ☐ a) evil ☐ b) angel ☐ c) good ☐ d) ban	2) WET ☐ a) appetite ☐ b) strong ☐ c) watery ☐ d) dry
3) CHIEF ☐ a) mainly ☐ b) minor ☐ c) head ☐ d) unimportant	4) CHOP ☐ a) rough ☐ b) duty ☐ c) stormy ☐ d) divide
5) SOFT ☐ a) harsh ☐ b) undemanding ☐ c) contact ☐ d) comfort	6) GOWN ☐ a) sack ☐ b) shout ☐ c) robe ☐ d) about
7) IMAGINARY ☐ a) realistic ☐ b) bleak ☐ c) trance ☐ d) dreamy	8) ACTIVE ☐ a) mobile ☐ b) baffle ☐ c) rigid ☐ d) motion
9) PIERCE ☐ a) puncture ☐ b) stung ☐ c) loud ☐ d) stabbing	10) INVALUABLE ☐ a) worthless ☐ b) valuable ☐ c) variable ☐ d) cheap

11) ADAPT	12) IMPARTIAL
☐ a) convert ☐ b) flexible ☐ c) inflexible ☐ d) transformation	☐ a) connected ☐ b) detached ☐ c) involved ☐ d) unconcern
13) REPUTABLE ☐ a) infamous ☐ b) supposed ☐ c) good ☐ d) stature	**14) LIGHTEN** ☐ a) discover ☐ b) darken ☐ c) illumine ☐ d) weak
15) GROUNDLESS ☐ a) justified ☐ b) background ☐ c) basis ☐ d) absurd	**16) FASTEN** ☐ a) affix ☐ b) untie ☐ c) holder ☐ d) thin
17) BARGAINING ☐ a) trafficking ☐ b) anticipate ☐ c) promise ☐ d) agree	**18) WORRISOME** ☐ a) reassuring ☐ b) unworried ☐ c) annoy ☐ d) perturbing
19) UNDERCURRENT ☐ a) undercharge ☐ b) atmosphere ☐ c) undermine ☐ d) belittle	**20) SATANIC** ☐ a) divine ☐ b) devil ☐ c) inhuman ☐ d) biting

21) PRICELESS ☐ a) prized ☐ b) cheap ☐ c) menu ☐ d) expense	22) MUTINOUS ☐ a) defiance ☐ b) uprising ☐ c) obedient ☐ d) turbulent
23) HOMELY ☐ a) mother ☐ b) domestic ☐ c) formal ☐ d) revered	24) FUNCTIONAL ☐ a) plain ☐ b) official ☐ c) decorative ☐ d) gathering
25) EXEMPT ☐ a) spared ☐ b) liable ☐ c) except ☐ d) illustrate	26) GALLANT ☐ a) cowardly ☐ b) escort ☐ c) courageousness ☐ d) polite
27) EXPRESSLY ☐ a) assert ☐ b) energetic ☐ c) particularly ☐ d) vaguely	28) DAPPER ☐ a) sloppy ☐ b) spry ☐ c) bespeckled ☐ d) dappled
29) COGNISANT ☐ a) unaware ☐ b) apprehension ☐ c) acquainted ☐ d) perception	30) PORTEND ☐ a) presage ☐ b) insignificant ☐ c) presentiment ☐ d) emblazon

31) BENEDICTION	32) CONCOMITANT
☐ a) anathema	☐ a) coincidental
☐ b) benevolence	☐ b) accidental
☐ c) munificence	☐ c) incidental
☐ d) blessing	☐ d) compressed
33) GUILELESS	**34) CULMINATE**
☐ a) artful	☐ a) crown
☐ b) shame	☐ b) peak
☐ c) innocent	☐ c) begin
☐ d) transparent	☐ d) pursue
35) EXONERATE	**36) ICONOCLASTIC**
☐ a) absolution	☐ a) denunciatory
☐ b) inflate	☐ b) credulity
☐ c) incriminate	☐ c) uncritical
☐ d) vindicate	☐ d) optimistic
37) IMPLICIT	**38) PENURIOUS**
☐ a) innuendo	☐ a) paucity
☐ b) explicit	☐ b) indigent
☐ c) latent	☐ c) dearth
☐ d) stated	☐ d) meditative
39) SPURIOUS	**40) TRANSMOGRIFY**
☐ a) authentic	☐ a) attitudinise
☐ b) specious	☐ b) traverse
☐ c) sordid	☐ c) mutation
☐ d) dishevelled	☐ d) metamorphose

Answers

1. a	9. a	17. a	25. a	33. c
2. c	10. b	18. d	26. d	34. b
3. c	11. a	19. b	27. c	35. d
4. d	12. b	20. c	28. b	36. a
5. b	13. c	21. a	29. c	37. c
6. c	14. c	22. d	30. a	38. b
7. d	15. d	23. b	31. d	39. b
8. a	16. a	24. a	32. c	40. d

Scoring

Number right minus number wrong = __________

Plus 2 aged under 16, plus 1 if aged 17–20 + __________

Score on the test = __________

Use the following table to convert your test score to a score out of 10 or 'sten score'. You can then enter your 'sten score' in the chart on page 200.

Test score	1–3	4–6	7–9	10–13	14–17	18–22	23–25	26–28	29–31	32+
Sten score	1	2	3	4	5	6	7	8	9	10

Test 21

Verbal precision

This test is to see how well you understand words and whether you can use them correctly. You are given a word or a pair of words. You have to select the word that fits best from the alternatives given. For each question there are alternative answers. Underline the correct answer. The first one has been done to show you how.

Examples

1. Which word has the closest meaning to Grave?

   a) Serious b) Gravity c) Needy d) Detain

2. Which word is most nearly the opposite to Retreat?

   a) Study b) Defend c) Advance d) Walking

In Example 1, of the options given, the word that is nearest in meaning to 'grave' is 'serious' so a) is underlined. In Example 2, the answer is c) 'Advance'.

In Example 1, 'grave' can have more than one meaning. It can mean where someone is buried, for example. It can also mean 'to scrape out', although this meaning is not used much these days. But if you look at the alternative answers, a) to d), none of these has to do with where a person is buried and none means 'to scrape'. 'Serious' means solemn, purposeful or important. 'Gravity' can also mean solemn or important, but can also have to do with the force than brings things to earth. 'Needy' has nothing to do with 'grave' because 'needy' means 'poor'. Although being 'needy' might be a 'grave' matter, it does not actually mean the same since being poor is not necessarily also serious. 'Detain' means to keep back or withhold, so does not have a similar meaning to 'Grave'. So, of the alternatives, it seems that 'grave' could go with 'serious', but might also share a similar meaning to 'gravity'. How do you decide between 'serious' and 'gravity'? 'Grave' can be used as a describing word as can 'serious'. Therefore, they are both being used as adjectives, whereas 'gravity' is the name of something. 'Gravity' can only be used as a noun. Therefore, 'grave' has the closest meaning to 'serious', so a) is the answer.

In Example 2, the opposite of 'retreat' would be to 'go forward' or 'advance'. 'Study' means something different. 'Defend' could be connected in some way with 'retreat', but is not the opposite. 'Walking' could describe both the manner of an 'advance' or a 'retreat'. It is not connected and neither is it the correct part of speech. Therefore, of the alternatives given, 'advance' is most nearly the opposite of 'retreat', so c) is the answer.

Do not mark this book if it is not your own, but record your answers and any working out you need to do on separate paper. If you wish to gain an estimate of your aptitude, record the number of the question you are on after exactly 8 minutes. Otherwise, take as long as you wish to complete the items.

Timed test: 8 minutes

1. Which word has the closest meaning to Seek?
   a) Lose b) Pursue c) Hide d) Cover

2. Which word is most nearly the opposite to Constant?
   a) Soon b) Unpredictable c) Approved d) Continual

3. Which word is closest in meaning to Majority?
   a) Legal b) Minority c) Old d) Most

4. Which word is closest in meaning to Ripe?
   a) Fruit b) Ready c) Aged d) Spoiled

5. Which word is closest in meaning to Recover?
   a) Restore b) Lose c) Conscious d) Make

6. Which word is closest in meaning to Envelop?
   a) Post b) Wrap c) Letter d) Show

7. Which word is most nearly the opposite in meaning to Hinder?
   a) Former b) Intercept c) Encourage d) Anticipate

8. Which word is most nearly the opposite of Gangling?
   a) Soft b) Quiet c) Skinny d) Dumpy

9. Which word is closest in meaning to Captivate?
   a) Partner b) Battle c) Remove d) Charm

10. Which word is closest in meaning to Obscure?
    a) Parasol b) Cloud c) Clear d) Blind

11. Which word is most nearly the opposite of Casual?
    a) Feeble b) Charming c) Deliberate d) Weak

12. Which word is closest in meaning to Catcall?
    a) Praise b) Scream c) Whistle d) Ovation

13. Which word is most nearly the opposite of Prohibit?
    a) Refuse b) Smoke c) Untrue d) Allow

14. Which word is closest in meaning to Cast?
    a) Class b) Tinge c) Species d) Barrel

15. Which word is closest in meaning to Debut?
    a) Termination b) Young c) Premiere d) Speech

16. Which word is most nearly the opposite of Buoyant?
    a) Rising b) Floating c) Sinking d) Marking

17. Which word is closest in meaning to Flotilla?
    a) Swans b) Ships c) Heart problem d) Balloons

18. Which word is closest in meaning to Crown?
    a) Adorn b) Cross c) Hill d) Jewel

19. Which word is most nearly the opposite of Gusto?
    a) Fame b) Desire c) Apathy d) Appetite

20. Which word is closest in meaning to Saucy?
    a) Lippy b) Politeness c) Container d) Interference

21. Which word is closest in meaning to Phoenix?
    a) Bird b) Statue c) Phony d) Fire

22. Which word is closest in meaning to Ambrosia?
    a) Food b) Dainty c) Jam d) Crab

23. Which word is closest in meaning to Developed?
    a) Ungrudging b) Generous c) Cultivated d) Boundless

24. Which word is closest in meaning to Ridiculous?
    a) Levity b) Jocular c) Wit d) Foolish

25. Which word is most nearly the opposite of Bent
    a) Bias b) Curved c) Leaning d) Impartiality

26. Which word is closest in meaning to Manual?
    a) Primer b) Note c) Voucher d) Disk

27. Which word is closest in meaning to Catch?
    a) Entangle b) Extricate c) Unravel d) Sprawl

28. Which word is most nearly the opposite of Imprudent?
    a) Arbitrary b) Judicious c) Undiscerning d) Subjective

29. Which word is closest in meaning to Retain?
    a) Dole b) Mete c) Portion d) Keep

30. Which word is most nearly opposite to Loathing?
    a) Doting b) Bungling c) Hiding d) Kindness

Answers

1. b	7. c	13. d	19. c	25. d
2. b	8. d	14. b	20. a	26. a
3. d	9. d	15. c	21. a	27. a
4. b	10. b	16. c	22. a	28. b
5. a	11. c	17. b	23. c	29. d
6. b	12. c	18. a	24. d	30. a

Scoring

Number right minus number wrong = __________

Plus 2 aged under 16, plus 1 if aged 17–20 + __________

Score on the test = __________

Use the following table to convert your test score to a score out of 10 or 'sten score'. You can then enter your 'sten score' in the chart on page 200.

Test score	1–2	3–4	5–6	7–9	10–12	13–15	16–17	18–19	20–21	22+
Sten score	1	2	3	4	5	6	7	8	9	10

Calculating your IQ

The IQ (intelligence quotient) scale is a familiar 'measuring stick' or 'ruler'; it allows a comparison with any other individual or with any other reference group. The use of IQ, or percentiles, which is equally easy for most people to understand, locates your performance on a scale that is the same for everyone.

Any particular test score makes little sense by itself. It has to be compared with a relevant population. A population may be any class of people, animals or objects that may be defined as relevant. For example, in medicine it might be helpful to check on the development of a newborn baby by comparing the weight of the baby with that of other newborn babies. Over time, data become available for an enormous number of newly born babies, so the mean (average) weight becomes a highly accurate representation of the population of babies.

As more data are acquired it possible to become increasingly certain about how 'true' population statistics are. Because of the difficulty of testing large groups of people, statisticians and other researchers, including market researchers, often try to pinpoint a 'cross-section' of the entire population. Or they may target a particular population, such as a sample of twins, people in a certain income group or people who have passed accountancy examinations. For most tests, we refer to a sample of people who have taken the tests, referring to the sample as the 'population'. We make the assumption that the magnitude and variability of the sample is a true representation of the entire population, or the 'normal distribution'.

The normal distribution

If it were possible to test everybody in an entire population on a particular variable we assume that the scores would be dispersed about the mean in a characteristic way that we refer to as 'normal'. Any sample or set of scores is assumed to be part of the normal distribution.

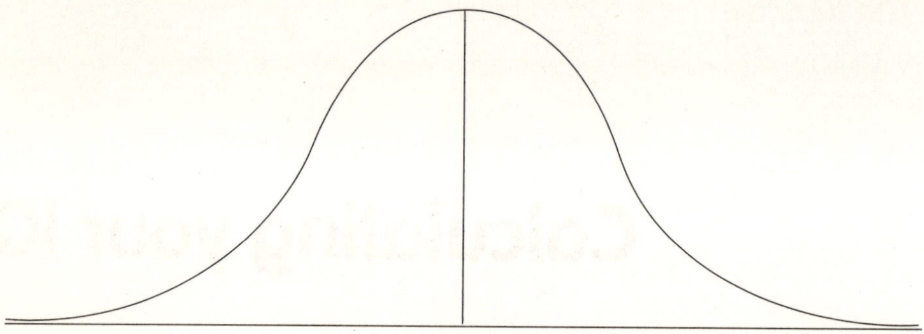

In the curve of normal distribution the base line represents the variable in question. It is usual to place the lowest number in the scale on the left side and the highest on the right. The highest point on the curve shows the mean or average point. So the greatest number of scores will be at the greatest magnitude. The mean could be drawn as a vertical line from the highest point down to the base line. About the mean, the two curves, that is, one on the left and one on the right of the mean, are symmetrical so that there is an equal magnitude of scores on both sides of the curve. Beneath any point on the curve the relative quantity or density of scores at that magnitude can be represented. Using the normal distribution allows us to place different sets of data on the same scale.

In this book effort has been made to include tests that will as far as possible reflect the curve of the normal distribution. In other words, the test gets harder as you proceed through it! At the end of each test, your result may be compared by reference to the chart of normal distribution.

Comparing your scores using the IQ

Your IQ is a number by which you can a) compare yourself with other people on any tests, and b) compare your own performance between the tests.

This book cannot measure your IQ with any great accuracy, as the conditions for measuring your IQ, as well as the information required to compare your intelligence with a satisfactory sample of people like you, are not available.

Why, then, provide a guide to IQ? First, because you are likely to find the exercise interesting for its own sake. Secondly, because the tests in this book are very similar to other tests used to measure intelligence, it enables a fuller comprehension of the entire process of intellectual measurement. Furthermore, an estimate of IQ provides a quick way of asking yourself whether you are going in a direction with your studies or in your career that will allow you to fully use your potential.

The IQ scale

Most IQ scales use the number 100 as an average. People with above average scores, say, above about 115 on appropriate tests, usually extend their schooling, obtaining vocational and technical qualifications.

People with stronger aptitudes are usually able to apply themselves to degree or professional courses. This group will, roughly, be the intellectual top 10 per cent and have an average IQ of 119. The top 5 per cent have an IQ around 125. If you are very good at the tests, you may have an IQ that is around 135, which puts you into the top 1 per cent.

Remember to interpret your own score only as a general guide. Your 'true' IQ will not be revealed unless you are compared with people of the same age, sex and relevant background. It is best to assume that your own IQ from the table provided here is likely to be only a baseline estimate. Use it to ask yourself whether you are achieving what you would expect at college or in your career. What tests should you use to calculate your IQ? It is possible to obtain an IQ on each one of the tests. The fairest estimate is probably to take the sum of several scores, then divide that number by the number of tests you have used.

Find your IQ by using the chart on the next page. Use your score out of 10 on any test and relate this to the IQ figures at the top.

IQ	100	105	110	115	120	125	130	135	140	145
ABSTRACT VISUAL										
1. Constructs	1	2	3	4	5	6	7	8	9	10
2. Sequences	1	2	3	4	5	6	7	8	9	10
3. Perceptual	1	2	3	4	5	6	7	8	9	10
ABSTRACT NUMERICAL										
4. Reasoning	1	2	3	4	5	6	7	8	9	10
5. Interpolation	1	2	3	4	5	6	7	8	9	10
ABSTRACT VERBAL										
6. Deduction	1	2	3	4	5	6	7	8	9	10
7. Analysis	1	2	3	4	5	6	7	8	9	10
MECHANICAL										
8. Dynamics	1	2	3	4	5	6	7	8	9	10
9. Tracing	1	2	3	4	5	6	7	8	9	10
SPATIAL										
10. Formation	1	2	3	4	5	6	7	8	9	10
11. 3D tests	1	2	3	4	5	6	7	8	9	10
PRACTICAL NUMERICAL										
12. Reckoning	1	2	3	4	5	6	7	8	9	10
13. Arithmetic	1	2	3	4	5	6	7	8	9	10
14. Figure work	1	2	3	4	5	6	7	8	9	10
15. Numbers	1	2	3	4	5	6	7	8	9	10
16. Calculations	1	2	3	4	5	6	7	8	9	10
SYSTEMS										
17. Systems	1	2	3	4	5	6	7	8	9	10
18. Coding	1	2	3	4	5	6	7	8	9	10
PRACTICAL VERBAL										
19. Word usage	1	2	3	4	5	6	7	8	9	10
20. Vocabulary	1	2	3	4	5	6	7	8	9	10
21. Verbal precision	1	2	3	4	5	6	7	8	9	10

As it can be misleading to try to calculate IQ from the score of a single test, use the following method to measure more accurately by using a number of tests, thus including some different aspects of intelligence. The chart is not absolutely accurate; because of the reasons given above and in the Introduction, it only intends to provide approximate guidance.

Calculating your overall IQ

(The space is for entering the number of tests used.)

Add sten scores from (______) tests = __________

Divide by (______) tests = __________

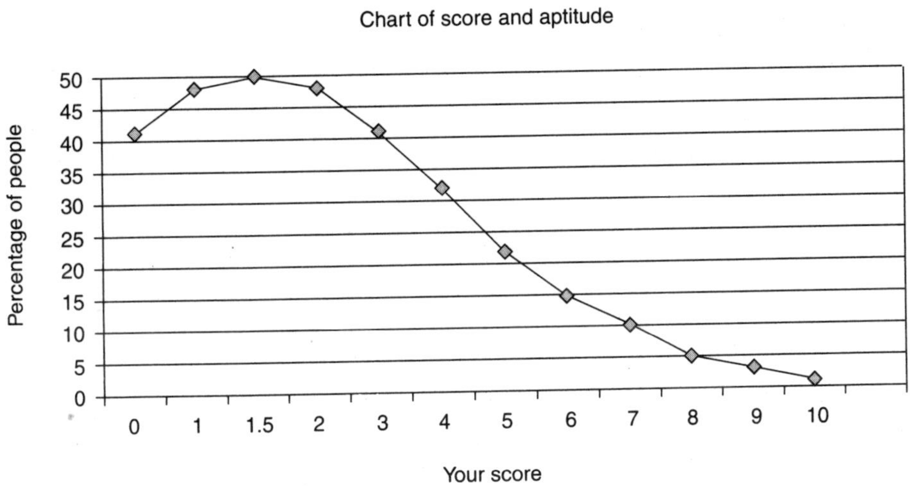

IQ 95 98 100 102 105 110 115 118 120 125 130 135 140

Explanation: if, for example, you scored 7, only 10 per cent of people scored more highly; you are in the 'top 10 per cent' and the equivalent IQ is 120.